Newman
10101
(PASADENA)

To Dorothea
Xmas greetings & love
from May & Dolly

Xmas 1946

THE FLASH BY TWO TREES—WHITEFRONTS

by PETER SCOTT

COUNTRYSIDE CHARACTER

Compiled by

RICHARD HARMAN

BLANDFORD PRESS

LONDON

First Edition September 1946

Set and printed in Great Britain by
Tonbridge Printers Ltd. Peach Hall Works,
Tonbridge, Kent
and Published by
Blandford Press Ltd. 16 West Central St.
London, W.C.1

Contents

	Page
THE HOUSE OF SECRETS (*Daphne du Maurier*) . . .	9
THE CLODHOPPERS (*Henry Williamson*)	18
PRINCE (*Adrian Bell*)	35
WOLD SHEP (*A. G. Street*)	50
PORTRAIT OF A DALESMAN (*Harry J. Scott*) . . .	60
THE SPIRIT OF BRITAIN (*Kenneth Belden*). Illustrated *facing page* 72
THE COAST OF ENCHANTED WINGS (*J. Wentworth Day*) .	105
THE CHAIR-MAKER (*H. J. Massingham*)	121
AMERICAN UNCLES (*Peter Howard*)	136
THE HERON AT HOME AND AT WORK (*Frances Pitt*) . .	148
THE CALL OF THE TREES (*S. L. Bensusan*) . . .	165
HILLS OF ENCHANTMENT (*Helen Hardinge*) . . .	177
SALINE MIXTURE (*Lord Mottistone*)	191
A HOUSE SET ON A HILL (*Irene Prestwich*) . . .	199
TIME AND THE WELSH MOUNTAINS (*Rhys Davies*) . .	209
"CY" (*Walter Rose*)	220
THE TEN-POINTER (*Richard Clapham*) . . .	228

Compiled by Richard Harman

Illustrations by Joan Rickarby

PHOTOGRAPHIC SECTION

Acknowledgments are made to the following:—

Joan Muspratt, Helen Muspratt, Dorothy Peters, J. Hardman, Eric Guy, Positive Pictures, Fox Photos, Keystone Press Agency, The British Council.

Also to G. Bell & Sons Ltd. for permission to reproduce "The Downs East of Steyning Round Hill" from "Pocket Guide to Sussex."

In our time Peter Scott follows in succession
a line of masters who have expressed their feeling
for the countryside with the brush.

The two pictures reproduced—

The Flash by Two Trees—Whitefronts
Floating on to the Merse—Barnacles,

were painted in 1945 for *Countryside Character.*

Foreword

I SUPPOSE that the love for the countryside which exists in everyone's heart springs from the fact that however much political, economic and social conditions may change, nature and her laws remain.

So fast do we move in this atomic age that we welcome an escape from its pace, and cherish the abiding and steadfast values which are found in things eternal.

Those who would appreciate the British countryside to its full must look deep. The contemplation of a lovely valley, the thrill of mountain scenery, the peace of the Thames below Marlow, the contented " all's-well-with-the-world " feeling in well-farmed fields are but a partial experience. Something lies much deeper; there is a soul which lives in the soil itself and a spirit we shall learn to know if we are wise.

I speak from experience. As a boy my home was in a large Cambridgeshire village which was typical of thousands throughout the length and breadth of this country. The people worked on the land and were interested in the land. From Monday morning to Saturday night they were at their job, and Sunday too, if they were shepherds or stockmen.

The boys looked to the day when they would leave school and start alongside their fathers. Already they spent their Saturdays hoeing fields, pulling charlock or chaff-treading for sevenpence a day. In August and September all worked in the harvest field, and earned money to buy their clothes for the coming year. The school holidays were regulated according to whether the harvest was late or early. The chairman of the school managers, a farmer, had the final say as to the breaking up day, and the other farmers complained that his crops were always late and that, consequently, the school never broke up early enough. The women and younger children gleaned the fields, many gathering sufficient corn to last them through the winter. At a harvest thanksgiving service a local preacher, referring to horse raking, complained that a new farmer in the district was so commercially minded that he went over his fields with a small tooth comb and left nothing for the gleaners.

The community spirit in those villages was greater than will ever be bred in any modern palatial community centre. It was found in the pub, or the village club, in the well-attended meetings on week-days in connexion with church or chapel, and the full congregations on Sundays. Whatever happened in the village—lecture, social or flower show, Easter Cantata or the feast—the whole village threw itself into the affair without reserve.

The feast, held on the first Saturday in July, was a traditional event going back to the years before memory. In the early days it was, of course, a trading event with the chapmen and cattle dealers. Later it became an affair of roundabouts and "Hoop-la." But one tradition remained. The menu for that Saturday mid-day dinner: roast pork, and gooseberry tart made from gooseberries nearly ripe and the redder the better. It was the one day of the year when the agricultural labourer claimed a special holiday.

Such was the connexion between land and people. They lived in thatched houses made of "brick bats"—straw and clay. All cropped big allotments, kept a pig, poultry and rabbits. Their wages were thirteen or fourteen shillings a week.

It was the time of lusty sport and tales were still told by the old folk of bare-fisted pugilistic encounters in former days. Cricket and football, each in its season, saw a real love of the game as well as a keen rivalry between village and village. Teams would walk, or cycle if they were fortunate owners of machines, some miles to the next village, play a hard game, and walk or cycle home again.

The men worked for the same employer, year in, year out. Each farmer's affairs were known to all. This one's over-fat pigs were always a subject for jest; ricks kept unthreshed, in the hope of higher corn prices became verminous and an object lesson in the folly of worldly wisdom; a very fine field of wheat grown by a small farmer was looked on with great admiration, but one whose fields became choked with weeds was known as a "thistle grower." Mostly they were sincere men who farmed well and gained respect. Those who did not live up to the best traditions of farming were looked upon with contempt.

I particularly remember one legal gentleman who acquired property with manorial rights which he exercised to the limit. Although a very mediocre player he took up cricket with enthusiasm, and because of his patronage was elected captain. He had his own private cricket pitch and nets and induced the

best bowler in the team to bowl at him once or twice a week
for practice. But when he found the bowler on some land with
ferrets he straightway prosecuted him in the local court. The
bowler's comment was that, having in mind the bowling
services he had rendered, he had never experienced such base
ingratitude!

Then I remember the patriarchal men, elders of the chapels,
men who seemed towers of strength. They were men with that
puritanical background which proclaimed, "Here are no weak-
lings." These men handed down the traditions or tales from
the time when Cromwell recruited and gathered his armies in
that part of England. They were often fathers of big families,
and what a credit these families were to the parents. On thirteen
shillings a week, families of twelve and more children were
reared, well turned out in neat, if much-patched clothes, a
testimony to the industry of the mother. No family would have
much, if anything, to spare in the way of money or possessions.
There were, of course, unhappy cases of families in difficulties,
but these were a small minority, and the parents were, for
reasons of self-neglect or drink, not typical of the average
villager.

And so life went on. The women gossiped across their gardens. Before the coming of the district nurse the local midwife
was also the school cleaner, and would be called straight from
stoking the boiler or washing the floor to a confinement. Hard
living did not allow much softness in these women, but their
hearts were warm with a kindness and a caring which was shown
in true neighbourliness, the bringing up of their children and
a deep concern for any child of the village.

This is an attempt to sketch life as it was in an ordinary
village before the flight from the land in the 1920's, and as it
had been for centuries. It is interesting to probe the four
hundred years up to that time, and discover that Britain's
country stock has contributed more lasting influence to the
world than any other.

The British Empire, the greatest the world has seen, was
largely populated by those pioneers who went out to the new
lands from the villages and farms of the homeland. The great
Dominions were stocked by the men and women of the English,
Scotch, Welsh and Irish countrysides. They carry on great
traditions side by side with us.

The Pilgrim Fathers, that revered group of a hundred and two persons who sailed from Plymouth in 1620, were bred and born in the farms and villages of England.

Spiritual strength is deeply rooted in every corner of this island, and history reveals that in the past four hundred years the nation's manpower, drawn from the yeoman, has stood rock-like in meeting every would-be world tyrant from Philip of Spain, Louis XIV and Napoleon, to the Kaiser, Hitler and Hirohito.

There is something deeper in the countryside than lovely scenes and picturesque farms and villages. There are the ways and conduct of men, and their manner and basis of life. There is a heritage built up over the centuries by the people who lived in closest touch with the world as it was created.

"You think a lot," said J. Wentworth Day to a shepherd he describes in *Farming Adventure*.

"If you spend all your life with the sheep under God's Heaven you *must* think, sir," replied the shepherd. "I've laid rough half my life. If you live like that, you know there's a God above."

Many famous authors have contributed to the collection in this book. In the course of their writing we shall find that they have sounded an accompaniment on the deeper notes of Countryside Character.

RICHARD HARMAN.

June, 1946.

FLOATING ON TO THE MERSE—BARNACLES   *by PETER SCOTT*

The House of Secrets

By Daphne Du Maurier

It was an afternoon in late autumn, the first time I tried to find the house. October, November, the month itself escapes me. But in the West Country autumn can make herself a witch, and place a spell upon the walker. The trees were golden brown, the hydrangeas had massive heads still blue and untouched by flecks of wistful grey, and I set forth at three of an afternoon with foolish notions of August still in my head. I will strike inland, I thought, and come back by way of the cliffs, and the sun will yet be high, or at worst touching the horizon beyond the western hills.

Of course, I was still a newcomer to the district, a summer visitor, whose people had but lately, within the year, bought the old "Swiss Cottage," as the locals called it, which name, to us, had horrid associations with an Underground railway in the Finchley Road at home.

We were not yet rooted. We were new folk from London.

We walked as tourists walked, seeing what should be seen. So my sister and I, pouring over an old guide-book, first came upon the name of Menabilly. What description the guide-book gave I cannot now remember, except that the house had been first built in the reign of Queen Elizabeth, that the grounds and woods had been in the last century famous for their beauty, and that the property had never changed hands from the time it came into being, but had passed down, in the male line, to the present owner. Three miles from the harbour, easy enough to find; but what about keepers, and gardeners, chauffeurs, and barking dogs? My sister was not such an inveterate trespasser as myself. We asked advice. "You'll find no dogs at Menabilly, not any keepers either," we were told, "the house is all shut up. The owner lives in Devon. But you'll have trouble in getting to the house. The drive is nearly three miles long, and overgrown."

I, for one, was not to be deterred. The autumn colours had me bewitched before the start. So we set forth, my sister more reluctant, with a panting pekinese held by a leash. We came to the lodge at four turnings, as we had been told, and opened the creaking iron gates with the false courage and appearance of bluff common to the trespasser. The lodge was deserted. No one peered at us from the windows. We slunk away down the drive, and were soon hidden by the trees. Is it really nigh on twenty years ago since I first walked that hidden drive and saw the beech trees, like the arches of a great cathedral, form a canopy above my head? I remember we did not talk, or if we did, we talked in whispers. That was the first effect the woods had upon both of us.

The drive twisted and turned in a way that I described many years afterwards, when sitting at a desk in Alexandria looking out upon a hard glazed sky and dusty palm trees, but on that first autumnal afternoon, when the drive was new to us, it had the magic quality of a place hitherto untrodden, unexplored. I was Scott in the Antarctic. I was Cortez in the Andes. Or possibly I was none of these things, but was a trespasser in time. The woods were sleeping now, but who, I wondered, had ridden through them once? What hoof-beats had sounded and then died away? What carriage wheels had rolled and vanished? Doublet and hose. Boot and jerkin. Patch and powder. Stock and patent leather. Crinoline and bonnet. . . .

The trees grew taller and the shrubs more menacing. Yet still the drive led on, and never a house at the end of it. Suddenly my sister said, "It's after four . . . and the sun's gone." The pekinese watched her, his pink tongue lolling. And then he stared into the bushes, pricking his ears at nothing. The first owl hooted. . . .

"I don't like it," said my sister firmly, "let's go home."

"But the house," I said with longing, "we haven't seen the house."

She hesitated, and I dragged her on. But in an instant the day was gone from us. The drive was become a muddied path, leading to nowhere, and the shrubs, green no longer but a shrouding black, turned to fantastic shapes and sizes. There was not one owl now, but twenty. And through the dark trees, with a pale grin upon his face, came the first glimmer of the livid Hunter's moon.

I knew then that I was beaten. For that night only.

"All right," I said grudgingly, "we'll find the house another time."

And following the moon's light we struck out through the trees and came out upon the hill-side. In the distance below us stretched the sea.

Behind us the woods and the valley through which we had come. But nowhere was there a sign of any house. Nowhere at all.

"Perhaps," I thought to myself, "it is a house of secrets, and has no wish to be disturbed." But I knew I should not rest until I had found it.

If I remember rightly the weather broke after that day, and the autumn rains were upon us. Driving rain, day after day. And we, not yet become acclimatized to Cornish wind and weather, packed up and returned to London for the winter. But I did not forget the woods of Menabilly, nor the house that waited. . . .

We came back again to Cornwall in the spring, and I was seized with a fever for fishing. I would be out in a boat most days, with a line in the water, and it did not matter much what came on the end of it, whether it would be seaweed or a dead crab, as long as I could sit on the thwart of a boat and hold a line and watch the sea. The boatman sculled off the little bay called Pridmouth, and as I looked at the land beyond and saw the massive trees climbing from the valley to the hill, the shape of it all seemed familiar.

"What's up there, in the trees?" I said.

"That's Menabilly," came the answer, "but you can't see the house from the shore. It's away up yonder. I've never been there myself." I felt a bite on my line at that moment and said no more. But the lure of Menabilly was upon me once again.

Next morning I did a thing I had never done before, nor ever did again, except once in the desert, where to see sunrise is the peak of all experience. In short, I rose at five a.m. I pulled across the harbour in my pram, walked through the sleeping town, and climbed out upon the cliffs just as the sun himself climbed out of Pont hill behind me. The sea was glass. The air was soft and misty warm. And the only other creature out of bed was a fisherman, hauling crab-pots, at the harbour mouth. It gave me a fine feeling of conceit, to be up before the world. My feet in sand-shoes seemed like wings. I came down to Pridmouth bay, passing the solitary cottage by the lake, and opening a small gate hard by, I saw a narrow path leading to the woods. Now, at last, I had the day before me, and no owls, no moon, no shadows could turn me back.

I followed the path to the summit of the hill, and then emerging from the woods turned left, and found myself upon a high grass walk, with all the bay stretched out below me, and the Gribbin head beyond.

I paused, stung by the beauty of that first pink glow of sunrise on the water, but the path led on, and I would not be deterred. Then I saw them for the first time—the scarlet rhododendrons. Massive and high they reared above my head, shielding the entrance to a long smooth lawn. I was hard upon it now, the place I sought. Some instinct made me crouch upon my belly and crawl softly on the wet grass to the foot of the shrubs. The morning mist was lifting, and the sun was coming up above the trees even as the moon had done last autumn. This time there was no owl; but blackbird, thrush, and robin greeting the summer day.

I edged my way on to the lawn, and there she stood. My house of secrets. My elusive Menabilly. . . .

The windows were shuttered fast, white and barred. Ivy covered the grey walls, and threw tendrils round the windows.

The house, like the world, was sleeping, too. But later, when the sun was high, there would come no wreath of smoke from the chimneys. The shutters would not be thrown back, nor the doors unfastened. No voices would sound within those darkened rooms. Menabilly would sleep on, like the sleeping beauty of the fairy tale, until someone should come to wake her.

I watched her awhile in silence, and then became emboldened, and walked across the lawn and stood beneath the windows. The scarlet rhododendrons encircled her lawns, to south, to east, to west. Behind her, to the north, were the tall trees and the deep woods. She was a two-storied house, and with the ivy off her would have a classical austerity that her present shaggy covering denied her.

One of her nineteenth-century owners had taken away her small-paned windows and given her plate glass instead, and he had also built at her northern end an ugly wing that conformed ill with the rest of her.

But with all her faults, most obvious to the eye, she had a grace and charm that made me hers upon the instant. She was, or so it seemed to me, bathed in a strange mystery. She held a secret—not one, not two, but many—that she withheld from many people, but would give to one who loved her well.

As I sat on the edge of the lawn and stared at her I felt like many romantic foolish people have felt about the Sphinx. Here was a block of stone, even as the desert Sphinx, made by man for his own purpose—yet she had a personality that was hers alone, without the touch of human hand.

One family only had lived within her walls. One family who had given her life. They had been born there, they had loved, they had quarrelled, they had suffered, they had died. And out of these emotions she had woven a personality for herself, she had become what their thoughts and their desires had made her.

And now the story was ended. She lay there in her last sleep. Nothing remained now for her but to decay and die. . . .

I cannot recollect now, how long I lay and stared at her. It was past noon perhaps when I came back to the living world. I was empty and light-headed, with no breakfast inside me. But the house possessed me from that day, even as a mistress holds her lover.

Ours was a strange relationship for fifteen years. I would put her from my mind for months at a time, and then, on coming again to Cornwall, I would wait a day or two, then visit her in secret.

Once again I would sit on the lawn and stare up at her windows. Sometimes I would find that the caretaker at the lodge, who came now and again to air the house, would leave a blind pulled back, showing a chink of space, so that by pressing my face to the window I could catch a glimpse of a room. There was one room—a dining-room I judged, because of the long sideboard against the wall—that held my fancy most. Dark panels. A great fireplace. And on the walls the family portraits stared into the silence and the dust. Another room, once a library, judging by the books upon the shelves, had become a lumber-place, and in the centre of it stood a great dappled rocking-horse with scarlet nostrils. What little blue-sashed, romping children once bestrode his back? Where was the laughter gone? Where were the voices that had called along the passages?

One autumn evening I found a window unclasped in the ugly north wing at the back. It must have been intuition that made me bring my torch with me that day. I threw open the creaking window and climbed in. Dust. Dust everywhere. The silence of death. I flashed my torch on to the cob-webbed walls and walked the house. At last. I had imagined it so often. Here were the rooms, leading from one another, that I had pictured only from outside. Here was the staircase, and the faded crimson wall. There the long drawing-room, with its shiny chintz sofas and chairs, and here the dining-room, a forgotten cork-screw still lying on the sideboard.

Suddenly the shadows became too many for me, and I turned and went back the way I came. Softly I closed the window behind me. And as I did so, from a broken pane on the floor above my head came a great white owl, who flapped his way into the woods and vanished. . . .

Some shred of convention still clinging to my nature turned me to respectability. I would not woo my love in secret. I wrote to the owner of the house and asked his permission to walk about his grounds. The request was granted. Now I could tread upon the lawns with a slip of paper in my pocket to show my good intentions, and no longer crawl belly to the ground like a slinking thief.

Little by little, too, I gleaned snatches of family history. There was the lady in blue who looked, so it was said, from a side window, yet few had seen her face. There was the cavalier found beneath the buttress wall more than a hundred years ago. There were the sixteenth century builders, merchants and traders; there were the Stuart royalists, who suffered for their king; the Tory landowners with their white wigs and their brood of children; the Victorian garden-lovers, with their rare plants and their shrubs.

I saw them all, in my mind's eye, down to the present owner, who could not love his home, and when I thought of him it was not of an elderly man, a respectable justice of the peace, but of a small boy orphaned at two years old, coming for his holidays in an Eton collar and tight black suit, watching his old grandfather with nervous doubtful eyes. The house of secrets. The house of stories.

In the year of '37, married by now, I found myself in Alexandria, and because I was not happy in the glare of pseudo East, I shut my eyes and dreamt of Menabilly. The story that came of this was called "Rebecca," and was based on nothing and on no one. Yet in a sense I cannot now explain, even to myself, far less than to others, Menabilly was Manderley, and Manderley was Menabilly. They were the same. Yet they had no likeness. What might have been. . . . What could have been. . . . What in truth was not. . . .

Rebecca was written, but my house of secrets held her secret still. The war came, and my husband and I were now at Hythe, in Kent, and many miles from Cornwall. I remember a letter coming from my sister.

"By the way, there is to be a sale at Menabilly. Everything to be sold up, and the house just left to fall to bits. Do you want anything?"

Did I want anything? I wanted her, my house. I wanted every stick of furniture, from the Jacobean oak to the Victorian bamboo. But what was the use? The war had come. There was no future for man, woman, or child. And anyway, Menabilly was entailed. The house itself could not be sold. No, she was just a dream, and would die, as dreams die always.

In '43 a change of plans sent me back to Cornwall, with my three children. I had not visited Menabilly since the war began. No bombs had come her way, yet she looked like a blitzed building. The shutters were not shuttered now. The panes were broken. She had been left to die.

It was easy to climb now through the front windows. The house was stripped and bare. Dirty paper on the floor. Great fungus growths from the ceiling. Moisture everywhere, death and decay. I could scarcely see the soul of her for the despair. The mould was in her bones.

Odd, yet fearful, what a few years of total neglect can do to a house, as to a man, a woman. . . . Have you seen a man who has once been handsome and strong, go unshaven and unkept? Have you seen a woman lovely in her youth, raddled beneath the eyes, her hair tousled and grey?

Sadder than either, more bitter and more poignant, is a lonely house.

I returned to my furnished cottage, in angry obstinate mood. Something was dying, without hope of being saved. And I would not stand it. Yet there was nothing I could do. Nothing? There was one faint, ridiculous chance in a million. . . . I telephoned my lawyer and asked him to write to the owner of Menabilly and ask him to let the house to me for a term of years. "He won't consent for a moment," I said. "It's just a shot at random."

But the shot went home. . . . A week later my lawyer came to see me.

"By the way," he said, "I believe you will be able to rent Menabilly. But you must treat it as a whim, you know. The place is in a fearful state. I doubt if you could do more than camp out there occasionally." I stared at him in amazement. "You mean—he would consent?" I said. "Why, yes, I gather so," answered my lawyer.

Then it began. Not the Battle of Britain, not the attack upon the soft under-belly of Europe that my husband was helping to conduct from Africa, but my own private war to live in Menabilly by the time that winter came again. . . .

"You're mad . . . you're crazy . . . you can't do it . . . there's no lighting . . . there's no water . . . there's no heating . . . you'll get no servants . . . it's impossible!"

I stood in the dining-room, surrounded by a little team of experts. There was the architect, the builder, the plumber, the electrician, and my lawyer, with a ruler in his hand which he waved like a magic baton.

"I don't think it can be done. . . ." And my answer always: "Please, please, see if it can be done."

The creeper cut from the windows. The windows mended. The men upon the roof mortaring the slates. The carpenter in the house, setting up the doors. The plumber in the well, measuring the water. The electrician on a ladder, wiring the walls. And the doors and windows open that had not been open for so long. The sun warming the cold dusty rooms. Fires of brushwood in the grates. And then the scrubbing of the floors that had felt neither brush nor mop for many years. Relays of charwomen, with buckets and swabs. The house alive with men and women. Where did they come from? How did it happen? The whole thing was an impossibility in war-time. Yet it did happen. And the gods were on my side. Summer turned to autumn, autumn to December. And in December came the vans of furniture; and the goods and chattels I had stored at the beginning of the war and thought never to see again, were placed, like fairy things, about the rooms at Menabilly.

Like fairy things, I said, and looking back, after living here two years, it is just that. A fairy tale. Even now I have to pinch myself to know that it is true. I belong to the house. The house belongs to me.

From the end of the lawn where I first saw her that May morning, I stand and look upon her face. The ivy is stripped. Smoke curls from the chimneys. The windows are flung wide. The doors are open. My children come running from the house on to the lawn. The rhododendrons bloom for me. Clumps of them stand upon my piano.

Slowly, in a dream, I walk towards the house. It is wrong, I think, to love a block of stone like this, as one loves a person. It cannot last. It cannot endure. Perhaps it is the very insecurity of the love that makes the passion strong. Because she is not mine by right. The house is still entailed, and one day will belong to another. . . .

I brush the thought aside. For this day, and for this night, she is mine.

And at midnight, when the children sleep, and all is hushed and still, I sit down at the piano and look at the panelled walls, and slowly, softly, with no one there to see, the house whispers her secrets, and the secrets turn to stories, and in strange and eerie fashion we are one, the house and I.

The Clodhoppers

By Henry Williamson

When I bought a derelict Norfolk farm and saw its weedy
condition, its tired and tufty grass, its boggy roads and overgrown hedges, I determined to begin with it as a farm all over
again, regarding it almost as virgin land. All the old, weedy
grass must, as soon as practicable, go under the plough.
"Even those steep Home hills?" asked an old fellow with
ragged cap, tattered coat, and hands like roots, who was working on the farm when I bought it. "Yes, even the Home hills,
Jimmy," I said. "But no plough could do it, guv'nor!" he

protested. "You wait and see," I replied with the confidence of inexperience.

That was two years before the war broke out. A year later farmers were being encouraged to plough up grassland, with an offer of a ministerial grant of £2 an acre. When the war came, they were asked to plough up a million acres of grassland. Then the "target" (as the current saying went) was another million acres, and again a third. Still we had no time to attempt the Home hills. From being a pioneer, I felt myself to be a near-failure. Often I looked at the hills with a feeling near to despair: I would never get them done. How about those dozens of black, ancient thorns, which had to be cleared first? The soil was sandy: what use ploughing up that, what would it grow asked the old fellow, who had remained working on the farm.

I determined to get the soil analysed; that would, anyway, be a start, I told myself. So I wrote to the War Agricultural Committee, and the following week someone came to see us. We talked as we sat on the hills, looking at the distant marshes and the sea; we parted the grasses with our fingers, examining the dwarf flowers and the thin plants that made up the sward. I talked of oats growing there; he said a crop of rye might be taken off it; but as the soil was light and sandy, would it not be better to plough it early in March and re-seed with grass and clover seeds on the upturned sod, after it had been pressed down by heavy rollers, and harrowed, of course? He was thinking of milk from the new sward: as arable land it was doubtful. In my enthusiasm I said I did want to see corn growing there; to use it as arable for some years, in order to kill the thistles which otherwise would flourish in any new pasture. "I can't bear thistles," I said. "When it is eventually re-sown with grass, I want to see it clean and fresh." "Well," he said gently, and with tact, "Our usual difficulty is in persuading a farmer to plough up his grassland, but if you are keen on taking a crop off it, and think you can do so. . . ." He was a farmer's son, from Devon, and I had known his village well when I had lived in the West Country. He was keen, alert, and his ambition, he told me, was to farm himself one day. I have heard and read of various farmers complaining about officialdom of the various county War Agricultural Executive Committees, but speaking only of my own limited experiences, I have nothing but praise for our Norfolk committee.

There is an old saying in farming: "Break a field and make a man." I wondered if it had come about during the Napoleonic blockade of the Baltic, when Britain had to depend on her own corn for bread. The price of wheat rose in those times to 160 shillings a quarter of eight bushels, or five times the peace-time price. Corn in those days was dibbled into the land, put in by hand into holes nine inches apart, three grains to a hole. My farm in those days probably had sixty men working on it; it had but two when I bought it, and now, in 1941, it was employing seven, eight with myself.

Many of the grass fields ploughed up when Napoleon was likely to beat Britain had not been ploughed since those times; now they were to be turned over again in the Hitlerian war. For over a century many of the rich lands of England had been grass, fattening grazing bullocks in spring and summer. What more could a man or a Government want better than grass that fatted bullocks with beef, asked the inheritors of those pastures, when confronted with ploughing-up orders in 1941 or 1942. During this period I read many letters in *The Times* about the wisdom, or the foolishness, of such ploughings. Some declared that modern grasses, notably those bred by Sir George Stapledon in Wales, had more leaf and less stalk than the old. Some grew more quickly, others of the same family were bred to mature more slowly, thus providing a "bite" both early and late in the year. The opponents of the ploughing-up policy of the Government declared that their old pastures—carefully grazed and kept almost like lawns—contained herbs (otherwise weeds) which the cattle selected for eating as they felt the need for them; they insisted that a layer of the new improved grasses was too strong, causing indigestion, or "blowing," and "scouring." To this the new-grass enthusiasts replied that the new layers required as skilful grazing as the old pastures, though for different reasons. Once the grazing of the new grasses was understood, they stated, the new pastures would be, for their greater leaf growth, superior to the old. Where one bullock grew into good beef, two might now graze.

.   .   .   .   .

In my amateur way I understood the reluctance of good grassland farmers to destroy their established swards by plough-ing, for I had come from Devon, a county of lush pastures made by warm sunshine and nourished by frequent rains. Norfolk, however, was not a grazing county. Sixty-four inches of rain fell in Devon for twenty-two in Norfolk. The West Country was famous for its cream and beef, the Eastern Counties for malting barley, and for pheasants and partridges. The chicks of game birds survived in dry East Anglia because their tiny feet did not get balled with sticky soil, which in the West caused them to fall behind the mother birds and so to die of exposure. Owing to the rainfall and the warm airs upon some of the grazing fields of Devon I used to wander over in my youth, those lush pastures earned in rent for six months a sum that would have bought outright more than twice their acreage of East Anglian arable land. In the depth of the depression that had fallen on British farming, some freehold Norfolk farms in 1932, with Elizabethan houses and a dozen cottages, and five hundred acres of land, sold for £1,000, or £2 an acre including the buildings; whereas the best Devon grazing let for £5 an acre between April and September.

Devon is a warm county. The air is soft, and the speech is therefore soft; the rain falls and the sun shines, the Gulf Stream infiltrating across the Atlantic keeps the winters mild. The grass is green in the West when it is grey in the East. Now, in the peril of Britain standing alone against the conqueror of Europe, we were in danger of starving, so plough up the land, for Britain must feed her own people off her own land. Farmers in 1941, according to popular newspapers, were almost heroes!

Before the war, I used to get in my old Alvis open car and cross England from the coast of Norfolk to the coast of Devon in a day. I left the shining North Sea in the morning as the sun was rising beyond Sweden, and came towards evening to the emerald green fields of Devon lying under the vast glory of an Atlantic sunset. All day with the sun, running over more than three hundred miles of England.

The sun rose through the oaks and pines of the Home hills, it drove a stupendous shining furrow across heaven, it sank in glory beyond the western sea and Labrador; and hardly were the dull bars of the midsummer sunset quenched before the morning star was glowing in the east, leading up the sun again to shine upon me through the window of my hilltop hut.

In those days of comparative peace, in my journeys across England, whenever I stopped I heard the dialects varying with

the soils; from the shrill, hard, quick, clipped North Norfolk
speech of the east winds and sandy brecks, to the slow burring
voices of the rich-red soils of Devon. Yet in those pre-war days
the red soil was discernible only in occasional fields, where
roots were being grown to feed the cows in winter; otherwise
there was little ploughing in the West Country. Half a million
visitors every summer wanted half a million pounds and more
of Devonshire cream a week, and who was going to bother
about growing oats or barley bringing in a gross return of £5
an acre, costing all but four-fifths of that to grow, when an
acre of grass by the sea might yield £100 each summer as a
caravan site, or £50 in milk and cream? And if you were particularly easy going, and couldn't be bothered with milk or
visitors, your 100-acre farm was looked after by one man,
whose job it was to attend four score bullocks which would
fatten themselves merely by walking about and lying down to
chew the cud. Agricultural depression in Devon? Not likely!
There was no culture of the fields, and a corresponding absence
of culture in the villages; for hard work and art go together.

Why bother to cut the thistles even? Everyone had plenty
of money. Missus took in visitors, at four or five or even six
guineas a week, and they were well-satisfied, for they returned
year after year. The coastal districts were crowded. In the old
towns of Barnstaple and Bideford, on market day, the farmers
did their business, arriving in smart new cars and sitting hours
in the taverns, discussing everything except farming. The grass
grew; that was their farming. They had no complaints. Their
harrows and their ploughs rusted in the corners of fields,
hidden by nettles, or were perches for flea-ridden hens in the
broken-down linhays and barns.

Thus the period between the two Industrial Wars, usually
called Great; but when the second internecine struggle was on,
what a difference in the fields of England!

To get to Devon one had to go by train; my war-time ration
of petrol as farmer was eight gallons for three months. What
a change after five years of war! During the 1944 harvest,
which lasted until October, I saw sheaves of corn sprouting six
inches out of the ear, still standing in the swampy fields. The
year before I saw hundreds of acres of corn laid flat on the
ground: plants of oats and barley, overfed from the rich
ploughed turf, were unable to stand up on the stalks. Thus

field upon field of overfed corn which had to be cut with the scythe. And the view from my hilltop eyrie was over thousands of fields of yellow corn fading into the late summer haze of the West Country.

    .   .   .   .   .

In 1943 we were at last able to set about bringing our own Home hills into cultivation. The first thing we did was to clear what Jimmy called the "great old bull-thorns." These trees, which wore a mantle of creamy white blossoms in May, had endured the bitter winter winds of a century and more. They were gnarled and black of trunk, their spines and twigs growing thick, matted, and set with long thorns which left a blue mark in the hand or leg whose flesh they pierced. In May turtle doves pleached their raft-like nests in them, and the June air was a-throb with their gentle notes. I had many doubts about cutting down the white-thorns and decided to leave one here and there, the shapeliest trees, so that when the corn was rising green I might also see and smell the creamy blossom of the may. Now to begin! As usual, I was a little trepidant: the job was a big one. Sharpening my axe, I went out one morning to start. After I had thrown, shredded, and stripped the first tree—one with seven intergrown trunks—a morning's work, my muscles unused to the 7-lb. axe-head—I went home and over a pint of tea I thought that what was needed was one of the bulldozers that were levelling tens of thousands of hedges to make the numerous airfields around us. But such luxuries were not for small folk like myself, certainly not in war-time. So I thought to telephone the owner of a 60-year-old traction engine which used to travel about, threshing the corn-stacks of small farmers like myself who could not afford to own one themselves.

A few days later the cumbrous 15-ton machine arrived to chuff and chug sideways up the hill and affix a great steel hook, attached to a 50-ton-strain steel cable, to the first 'great old bull-thorn.' The strain was taken, the flywheel moved round slowly, the cable tautened and trembled, the engine chuffed suddenly, there was a shriek and a crack, and the trunk was hauled forward, splintered salmon-pink above the root. Lesser trees yielded and came out with most of their roots, to be dragged on their sides with two or three tons of soil at their bases, leaving a crater like one made by a small bomb, of the

kind dropped by Heinkels in 1940. Before all were on their sides
the cable snapped nineteen times, for sixty-four trees. And there
they were left for the soil on the mat of roots to dry and fall off,
from corn-drilling to sugar-beet hoeing. After which the annual
rush went on: to cut and stack the hay, then to harvest the
corn, and after that the dung-carting from the cattle yards—the
trodden straw of the last harvest made into muck in the winter—
and moonlight ploughing for the winter-wheat, before the rains
came, and also because we were late for the lifting of the sugar-
beet. No time that year to attend to the uprooted thorns of the
Home hills. The nettles and the thistles grew around them, for
now we could not run the cutter over the hills.

. . . . .

At least, I said to the boys at our long oak table at supper,
they will make a grand beacon if the war ends suddenly. Think
of it, the greatest bonfire in Norfolk, sixty-four dry thorns,
some with trunks eighteen inches thick, making a beacon to
blaze on our hills! But the war did not end that year, and when
at last I went to clear them the nettles had risen and seeded
twice around them. After the constant winds sweeping over
the hill, the wood was dry and hard for the axe. Bit by bit,
however, we got the main branches lopped off, the lesser
branches piled and burned, the limbs and trunks laid in neat
upright heaps to be carted to the circular saw. At last the hills
were cleared, except for a few trees which the engine-driver,
with his ragged lengths of cable tied together, had not dared
to tackle. Standing on the slope, the 15-ton engine might have
got out of control, or even turned over.

When we came to clear the edges round the hills we found
that thorns and brambles had spread in places as much as
twenty yards into the grass, from the original boundary. Within
that jungle I found the rusty remains of four barbed-wire fences,
each several yards from its predecessor. Brambles had covered
them, the homes of scores of rabbits which had spoiled the
grass during the neglectful twenty years between the wars. We
cleared the wire and fences, but the roots stayed in the ground,
most of them belonging to the harder blackthorn. We made
fires on the root-stubs, which had to be doused every evening,
because of the black-out, and re-lit every day. Even so, the roots
remained, and when I took the Ferguson tractor with the deep-

digger plough to rip up the worst area by the hedges, for a summer fallow, I had to avoid most of them. The furrows left were rough, heaps of roots of bramble and lesser thorns. The soil under the turf looked dead and dry, as though neither air nor rain had penetrated there for centuries. I could do no more that spring, for the time was come to drill the corn once more.

.   .   .   .

Sometimes during the summer I used to walk up the hill, my feet pressing on the old turf springy with rest-harrow and wild thyme, and frequently impressed by a strange thistle whose leaves were low on the grasses, in the shape of a star. Its flower was a purple-red, and grew lower than the grasses. Had a thousand generations of sheep taught that thistle its cunning habit of self-protection? In the old days of free wandering over field and moor in Devon I would have admired it and been glad that it was, as a small unit of life, enduring by its own strength and tenacity; but now, as a farmer dreaming of fine redpoll cattle grazing on the hill, I saw the legions of dwarf thistles only as enemies that had to be deracinated. There were other thistles, too—the creeping thistle and the tall spear-thistle. The creeping thistles were in colonies; even they found it hard to push their roots through the dense and dry inter-twined roots of the ancient turf. Thyme grew on the hill, with eyebright and sulphur-yellow cowslips; where the rabbits had scratched, the dove's-foot crane's-bill could bloom. In July the fragile harebells trembled on their slender stalks, azure as summer sky in the breezes of the uplands. But I had no time or inclination (as I have now in retrospect) to admire or identify myself with wild flowers or the birds which passed over the hill; I was a farmer, a man driven by the nature of his calling to desire only the sight of corn growing where it had never grown before.

Two winters previously some tanks had come on the hill and cut up the turf with their tracks, and in the following spring I had cultivated those torn places, leaving a loose tilth behind, on which I had broadcast a few handfuls of trefoil and ryegrass, before rolling the seeds in and forgetting them. Along these irregular bands of new land the thistles rose, tall and thick, and the trefoil and rye grass grew luxuriantly. That alone told me that I was right in my idea to put the old worn-out turf under the plough.

C

The fire-circles left by the burning of the uprooted thorns remained bare during the summer. Those headlands by the hedges which had been roughly cleared of the roots of brambles and blackthorns, lay in sullen weathered furrows. My small ewe-flock had been sold a year previously; fifty Oxford-Suffolk crosses had kept the grass down in previous years. I wanted to begin ploughing at once, but the hydraulic tractor had been broken, and sent away for repairs; and about this time something broke in me, and I too was sent away for repairs. So the hills were left to the winds and the flowers, to the kestrel that hovered over the plateau for mice and beetles, and the village cats which prowled on the slopes for rabbits; and the meaner men of the district who were poachers for the black market.

. . . .

There were about ten acres of the hills altogether, of varying slopes lying north, west, and south. The official trowel had prodded and scooped and the official bag had carried away for analysis a light sandy soil deficient in phosphate and possibly able to support one crop of rye. This opinion had been given before the thorns had been wrenched out with arboreal shrieks and groans. It was only when the root-craters were visible that I saw to my delight that below the shallow top-soil of sand was a brownish-red medium loam similar to that of the field over the eastern hedge. There were pockets of sand on the hills, for the rabbit burrows were yellow with it; there was also gravel, for on the western slope lay a saucer-like depression which was obviously an old pit covered by grass; but under most of it, not too deep for our plough, lay that brown loam! It was curious how the soil was sandy among the roots of the congested grasses. As I broke it up in my fingers—a blackish sandy mould—it occurred to me that this ancient colony of grasses had, during the centuries, eaten all the heart out of the soil, leaving only indigestible sand. None of the original clay had been left; only small grains of rock called sand amidst the wreckage of centuries of dead roots. Under that layer of compost a fine medium soil was lying, ready to be enlivened by sun and air and rain. Plough and re-seed directly on the upturned sod? And have the finest crop of thistles in the district? No, I would plough in the ordinary manner, cultivate all summer to kill the thistle roots, and drill with corn after a year on weed-free land!

The visitor from the War Agricultural Committee was, as usual, pleasant and considerate to this idea, but a suggestion was made: Why not utilize the thistles for silage? Young thistles so treated were not unpalatable, and if oats and peas were sown in early spring, they might be cut in early June, after which the seven duck-foot cultivator feet behind the hydraulic tractor would keep the stubble stirred throughout the hot dry months of July, August, and September, and thus wither the roots and fallow the soil in accordance with my original idea. Meanwhile, would we be able to plough those steep slopes? The village said No. But the village didn't know the powers of a hydraulic tractor invented by a Belfast engineer; a tractor that Harry Ferguson could not sell in Britain, but which, taken to America and shown to Henry Ford, at once found the recognition of one man of mechanical genius for another.

．　　　．　　　．　　　．

The ploughing of the Home hills was started on Armistice Day, 1943. The Ferguson tractor, bought in 1937, with one engine reconditioning during the years, and a new barrel casing to replace the one accidentally broken, was still as good as new. The plough was a ten-inch double furrow. I opened the first furrow along the plateau, running from east to west, and returning west to east. I was on top of the world; the village lay below, with its trees, flint walls, and red-tiled roofs. Afar was the blue line of the North Sea above the sandhills, and on the horizon sailed a convoy of small ships. I found myself singing as the bright breasts of the plough turned up the sod and cast it over. It was sandy soil just there, it was level, it was easy. I had begun what I had waited to do during seven long years. My eyes felt clear, the world was filled with colour. A cock pheasant flew over me with rocketting wings, and I turned to watch him glide into the wood behind, thinking of the pigeon-shooting there in the coming months. I had a hide against one of the oak trees, made of boughs and interlaced with branches; this year would be the first I had shot since 1938. There had been no time, otherwise energy, in the interval.

The mat of wild and ancient grasses certainly was tough. I was on the easiest part of the hill, yet even in bottom gear the engine needed all its compression. The little 15-cwt. tractor was Gulliver among the Lilliputians: hundreds of roots were protesting and holding against the shear and lift of coulter, share, and breast. Sometimes the furrow-wheel with its iron spuds turned thumpingly, as the resistance of an extraordinarily strong clump of roots held the plough shudderingly still. Jumping off, I found there were roots, long, thick, and dark, of rest-harrow, and immediately thought that this was how the wildflower (I did not like to call it weed, even to myself) with its pink pea-like blooms, had gotten its name in olden time. Rest-harrow, or stop-horse.

The tractor did not rest. A slight lift of the lever and the hydraulic oil-pump lifted the twin ploughs; it went forward again. Another touch of the lever set the points deeper once more. All the way we were held up by the roots of rest-harrow, which went deep into the loamy subsoil.

I saw that I could not hope to penetrate to the rich brown loam at the first ploughing. It took the engine all of its multiple synthetic horses to cut two furrows each seven inches deep. The furrow slices, too, were by no means tractable; I longed for mould-boards or plough-breasts of the old Norfolk 'olland shape, by which the slices would have been gouged up and screwed over nearly 180 degrees and laid flat. My furrow slices often wavered behind the tractor, before deciding to sit upright, the grassy edge at right-angles to the earth from which they had been torn. Never mind, I thought, snow and frost will subdue those obstinate furrows, and in the spring our new disc-harrows will chop them to bits and press them down. So I went on with my task, easy in mind. It was a warm day. The convoy on the sea horizon proceeded without the rolling bomb-reverberations we were used to, for now the tide of war had changed, and along the far coast of North Africa the German armies had hastened in retreat, passing over a thousand miles of sand which once had been the cornfields of a great empire long ago gone to ruin; to ruin, some said, because Rome in its urban pride had forgotten that the strength and virtue of a race was based on the fertility of its soil. Rape the earth, and human love is eventually purposeless.

In the days that followed, as I ploughed the tough turf of the hill, I wondered whether Dr. Johnson, had he been with me, would have discovered an original and ironic meaning in a phrase often used among farmers and labourers to describe a stubborn object which temporarily frustrates their strength and ingenuity. Rest-harrow might, on account of roots like tarred ropes, cause a pair of horses to rest, and the ploughman with them, in sympathy; but as any ploughman of virgin soil will tell you, an old sod is liable to do more things than merely arrest the forward movement of a plough. Toiling up a slope of one in four there was a report like a rifle shot, followed by a grating noise. The two-inch steel axle had broken suddenly. Six years of arduous work on the other hilly fields, often gouging 20-lb. flints out of a sea-laid chalky sub-soil never disturbed during the millions of years since the waves had receded, had crystallized the steel—broken its heart—so that in dying it had gone back to its ancestral crystals. Fortunately we had a spare half-axle, and my dejection was equalled by the confidence of my son, who came up the hill with the new Ford-Ferguson tractor drawing a trailer with jack, tool-roll, and spare axle. I left him and one of our men to it and strolled away, feeling myself to be a slacker, yet arguing that as the doctor had ordered me to go easy after my return from hospital, I would obey, and spend an hour or two as a naturalist. What a hope! The perfection dream was as a toxic in my blood; and, after all, the boy was only seventeen, and had no experience except that picked up from my erratic self. To my delight, when I returned the new axle was fitted, and almost at once I was going slowly up the steep slope again, in bottom gear, peering backwards over my right shoulder for the pleasure of watching the turf rising up and flopping over. Always my hand was on the hydraulic lever, to raise the ploughs should the furrow-wheel begin to 'scrap,' or race in the furrow, when the pull of the turf was greater than the 2,400-lb. pull of the tractor. Once the furrow seemed to scream, my heart jumped, but it was only a stone caught between rear-furrow wheel and scraper. At other times the furrow would smoulder; a dull red spark glowered there; smoke fumed out of the damp earth. This was when a flint-and-steel spark had ignited dry roots. Sometimes, for a reason I could not account for, a strip of turf reared up behind the plough in contortion. It hesitated and then, with the aid of gravity the old sod unrolled along its length, yard after yard, sometimes as much as fifteen yards, settling itself as it had lain originally, grassy side up once again.

While I was ploughing up and down the hill Jimmy walked slowly from where he had been milking the cows. He stared about him. I got off, throttled back the tractor, and gave him a cigarette.

"Well, Jimmy, what do you think of it?"

"Humph!"

"What does that 'Humph!' mean, Jimmy?"

He puffed at the cigarette.

"Yew bruk its back, di'n you?" he said presently.

"Yes," I said, "but that axle was already strained and shocked by the flints on Hilly Piece, years ago."

"It was an' all."

"Shall we get a crop off the Home hills, d'you think, Jimmy?"

"Yew might."

"I might?"

"An' yew might break your neck, too, I'm thinking, 'bor. Fare you well." And with this encouragement the old fellow walked away. I knew Jimmy did not approve of the old haw-thorns being pulled out; and as I clambered into the sack-covered iron seat again I thought of W. H. Hudson's story, "The Old Thorn," and the Wiltshire legend that only harm would come to one who hurt a whitethorn.

It was suddenly cold on the hill. The Arctic Circle air that usually stole over the land, about five o'clock, struck through my clothes. I walked to the sullen furrow, trying to heave it over with my arms, knowing that if it lay like that it would not rot, but live to grow with greater exuberance in the spring, stimulated by the nitrogen of the coming snow and the cutting of the old roots. Kneeling down, I soon found it was vain to try and heave over the dull resistance of many hundredweights. There the furrow slice lay, ten inches by seven inches by fifty feet, a strip unbroken, marked by two parallel lines showing where the disc-coulters had cut the turf. The black-headed gulls which had been following the ploughing, soaring and sweeping down on white narrow wings, with open red mouths screaming for lug-worm and wire-worm, now were drifting disconsolately in the upper air. They were finished for the day; their brethren had already flown away in silent V-formations to their roost in the sandhills. I felt suddenly hopeless, and getting on the tractor, took it downhill to the hovel or cart-shed where it stood during the night. Then I went home, slowly, thinking of the dead in the sands of Africa, in the snows of Russia, in the grey wastes of the Atlantic, among the far islands of the East. I recalled the young pilot of the Luftwaffe lying in hospital with broken legs and arm and other bullet wounds, and how he had thrust his knuckles into his mouth to stop any cry in his throat. Having refused a blood transfusion, he had died two days later, with hardly a sound. And every night young men of the R.A.F. were burning in the terrible roar of petrol flames.

I passed Jimmy in the village street, coming back with his week's rations, and his weekly ounce of tobacco, for it was pay-night. He was a queer old fellow: a year before, when a mine had exploded a mile away on the coast, with a terrific reverberation and a column of smoke above the woods, he had come running to where I had been ploughing beyond the sky-line, gasping out that he had heard it, and thought it was the tractor blowing up. Jimmy felt the land through his whole body, as his forefathers had for a dozen centuries; he did not trust machinery. "What's it all lead to, guv'nor? Why that!" and he pointed to the bombers, hundreds of them in the height of the sky, going slowly east over the darkening seas to the Rhineland.

.   .   .   .   .

The next day, making an early start to finish the job, I began by attempting to reverse those stubborn furrows. I tried to replough them by running down the steep slopes backwards, then stopping, dropping the ploughs once more, and going uphill again. In vain; the furrow-wheel sank in and churned impotently; or the slices curled up, reared, doubled, and broke, to choke coulter, mould-board, and frame, until I had to stop, dismount, and shove, kick, heave, push the tangled furrow-heap apart. What a mess, I thought, and remembered the injunction of the War Agricultural Committee to 'plough in a husbandlike manner.' Well, some husbands on occasions kicked, pushed, and swore, so perhaps after all I was carrying out the order literally.

Yet on the whole it was not a bad job. I do not think any other tractor, even a crawler, could have tackled those slopes. Certainly not horses with an ordinary plough, though a special match-plough, of the kind used in competitions, might have turned a few nice furrows until its share was blunted and 'wrung.' Some parts of the hills had to be ploughed sideways; these were the most difficult, for the tractor was often leaning over at an angle that made me wonder if it would topple, and

I fall underneath it. It was then that I longed for a Devon one-way plough and a pair of strong horses. I had in the past watched a man with such a team ploughing across the side of a hill which rose at an angle of forty-five degrees. He began at the bottom, and at the end of the first furrow turned round, threw over the other plough-breast, and ploughed back beside the furrow, creeping slowly up the hill, parallel to the bottom, all the way up.

While I was going slowly round the headland, to finish the job, the intermediate strips having been ploughed, the gulls which had been accompanying me suddenly flew up, and I saw six small boys on the sky-line. Richard, who was seven and the leader, explained that he had been trying to reverse the sullen furrows, and might his gang follow behind the tractor, and push back any furrow-slice before it made up its mind to fall the wrong way?

"You are like Blucher at the battle of Waterloo," I said. "You come when the work is over."

"We didn't know," said Rikky seriously.

"I'm only joking."

They fell on the obstinate turf with the eagerness of starlings, dropping on knees and pushing and heaving with teeth clenched. This was indeed Man wrestling with Brute Nature. After a while it became too arduous, so they turned it into a game, under Rikky, whose job it was, apparently, to stand above and with a wave of a stick (which was also a tommy-gun) lead his men down to the assault of the backsliding furrows.

It was not long before small hands and knees were grubby with soil, and their fertile minds had enlarged the scope of their operations. A conference was called to deal with the new idea, and so they departed from the wake of the tractor to the inside of a distant hen-house, their headquarters. The gulls, which had been waiting impatiently above the small boys, now swept down once more, and the scream and scramble for worms, mice, and insects was again audible through the exhaust of the engine.

There were a few more rounds of the headland to be done, then the ploughing of the Home hills would be accomplished. It was growing late, and weariness was upon me. The sun was disappearing in the west, small and smoky, when I started on the final round. Frost was already settled in the shade by the lower hedge; it was growing visibly whiter. The engine seemed to be noisier. Doubts came with my fatigue—had I been foolish ever to think of ploughing the Home hills, and how much more sensible it would have been to have remained a writer, to sit by a fire on a winter's day and be my own master of time, instead of the farm being always master. Yet one day all this experience would be valuable; writing based on fancy only was worthless, like white bread. And at least I knew the worth of these end-of-the-day thoughts. No more thinking; be patient; one more round, and the tractor left by the hedge, waterproof cloth tied over the aluminium body, water drained from the radiator into that old can left by the army. Only one more round and then the ploughman might homeward plod his weary way. Enough of such selfish indulgence! I was one of the most fortunate of men. I had a fire to sit by at night, while all over the world homeless men were enduring existence without horizon.

The last flights of starlings had gone across the grey sky; the last straggling gulls were passing over in silence to the sandhills.

I thought of the bottle of whisky in the drawer of the tallboy in the parlour; this night I would entertain myself to a drink. The bottle was six years old, the only bottle brought into the house in that time of sparseness and economy, while the farm was being restored to the standards of good husbandry. Or was this restraint due to a puritan complex, a fear of becoming dependent for stimulation on alcohol? After all, whisky was made from barley, and I grew barley, so was it not natural to drink whisky when one was fatigued by the growing of it? I knew that the puritan complex, driving the body to do things beyond its capacity, was part of the philosophy obsessing Europe, and that it came from early inhibitions, as well as from agonized contemplation of human frustration. So, in twilight charged with the thunder of the great bombers passing slowly east like blowflies heavy with eggs, I came towards the end of the last furrow.

In front of me, where a long snake of turf had curled back, something glimmered in the thickening twilight, and stopping the tractor, I got off and walked stiffly forward, to pause above a pair of delicate grey wings spread motionless on the frosting furrows. One of the black-headed gulls, alighting and dipping for a worm, had been caught by the back-curling furrow of my penultimate round, and its head was pressed under the earth. It lay still, as though resigned, or crucified, the wings outspread, with the soft grey pearly bloom of unruffled plumage as though floating immobile on the gross earth. The poor bird must surely be suffocated, after lying like that for twenty minutes, I thought, as I knelt to heave back the strip of turf. It was very heavy, and almost beyond my strength, but at last I got it free, expecting the head to be limp and crushed. As I held the fragile bird in my open hands, it raised its head, turned to look at me, and a feeble scream came from its red mouth. Then after a further rest it elbowed itself lightly into the air, and with slow strokes of those slender grey wings floated away into the dusk. And slowly I went down the twisted furrows to my fireside, to sit and rest among my children, to drink my whisky while a feeling of contentment came upon me.

In the next summer the Home hills were golden-brown with a thick and sturdy crop of oats; and in the summer following the oats were even stronger, with gold-greasy heads and dark brown stems.

Prince

By Adrian Bell

A hook breaks: just a hook of the plough trace, that connects
it to the pulling tree of the plough, and I take the length of
chain to the blacksmith to have a new hook welded on. He is
sitting on his anvil talking to a friend, while his mate hammers
shoes he has just forged upon the hooves of a van-horse.

Other agricultural casualties are in his forge: he mends the
iron bones of farming, from a little thing like a root-scraper
("Haven't seen one that shape for a long time") to the ribbed
skeleton of a horse-rake with buckled wheels. A horse ran
away with that: this water-cart shaft a tractor ran over: and
—hadn't you heard?—they've just taken poor old George to
the asylum: he's been tidy queer for the last twelve-month, and
his farm begin to show it. Good little place that was.

Of the three powers in farming to-day—muscle, piston and

mind—this last is lord. Or under-lord. As the soft flesh directs and rules the impassive iron, which at a mischance can crush it with less force than it takes to turn a furrow, so the even less material mind rules all. Which is nature's truth and mystery, whereby an acorn grows an oak and not a chrysanthemum.

For years that broken hook had taken the strain between muscle and clay. Iron is harder than either, but in the end they outwear it. A hook might serve as a symbol of farming, as it does to the Russians: a reaping-hook, a trace-hook, any hook. An old-fashioned sheaf or plough has become too nostalgic; poets abetting. "Drowsed by the fume of poppies." No, sir, but tension, counter-strain. Yet not wild struggle either: that is only seen when the tractor wallows or a horse is out of hand or over-taxed. That is not farming. Farming is the integration and order of these forces; a nibbling at the tremendous inertia of matter, that wins against it.

A spade in a man's hand, and a seventy-horse-power tractor are the only two implements that can turn earth to the depth of two feet. I saw the seventy-horse-power plough being carted away on a lorry, after ploughing a field which I had recently reclaimed from the wild. A single, extra-tough root had smashed it, fractured its iron stem. My sharp spade, digging a drain in the same field, bit its way through that root and severed it.

The power that rules the land: what is it? It is obvious when you go into a generating station that you are in the midst of power. The great machines are there to show it. To wield power under a roof and on a concrete foundation is one thing: to wield it under an open sky and upon a living earth is quite another. For that an especial sort of wisdom is required. A farmer stands in his field. To cultivate this with a tractor will take a quarter of the time taken to do it with horses. In an impatient age it is not easy to put aside impatience: and yet if the state of the soil requires it, impatience must be overcome. The farmer stirs the soil with his toe, while new and various powers wait on his word. He needs wisdom beyond that of his fathers.

To-day under the open sky, in the lonely-looking field, we are in a power-house.

This by way of prelude, which really should come at the end, because it is a summing-up of a season of work on this, my heavy-land farm. Between the broken hook and an unbroken horse came spring, summer, autumn—and now it is winter.

That hook was on Prince's plough-trace: it hitched him to the first load he pulled, gave him his first taste of work. That was not a plough, but a log of wood; to be precise, an old railway sleeper. The iron horse and the horse of flesh and blood have fortuitous inter-connections.

There is not much time for the breaking of colts in modern farming. Not much use for horses either, you might be led to infer from much that is talked and written about mid-twentieth-century farming. Yet my horse Boxer, whom I sold in a spring sale, fetched nearly £80, not because he was an unusual animal —he wasn't—but because I could guarantee him quiet and a good worker in all gears, though only six years old. There is competition for such a horse at a busy season. Colts of three years old, and half-broken horses of four years old, were to be had cheap. There is plenty of demand for the services of a good horse, but not for the trouble of him.

Horses have a language between themselves that a man may understand. When my old mare Kitty came home tired from the plough or the dung-cart, Prince would bound to meet her at the horse-yard gate. He would escort her to the stable, snapping playfully at her neck. "What have you been up to all this time, to get you in that sweat?" "Work." "What's work? You're always talking about work." "You wait, you'll see," said Kitty.

Time passed, and Prince laughed at the idea of work. The old horsekeeper did not seem to have any intention of making Prince work. Every morning the harness would be put on Kitty, and her tucked-up and rather drooping body expressed a deep sigh: "Why always me? Look at that fat, hefty young thing at your side." Prince pranced after her through the yard. "If you don't like it, why put up with it?" And Kitty put her ears back, showing the whites of her eyes. "You wait."

It seemed as though Prince might wait, and mock, for ever. Kitty had become a habit with the old horsekeeper, like the cobwebs on the ceiling that were never swept down, and the broken forks and the worn-out horse-collars, that were useless but never thrown away.

But one day another and a younger man followed the old horsekeeper into the stable. The horses were aware of a new presence in the gloom cast by the smoky old lantern. He listened to the old horsekeeper telling his old stories, but when there came a pause he spoke of things that must be done to-day and to-morrow.

He came not once or twice, but every day into the stable; and when all the old stories had been told, and the horsekeeper—whom we will call Jim—began telling them again, he would interrupt them at the first sentence with what must be done on this land to-day and to-morrow. To which Jim would retort, "There's plenty of time for that yet," and try to get going with the story again. But the new master would say, "I don't like farming a week behind the weather," and walk out.

Now in the old days there had not been a great deal of oats and hay on the farm, because the long stories had necessitated so many pauses, and there was always "plenty of time for that yet," till the time for sowing oats was past. Similarly, the time of reaping and the time of making hay were so drawn out that bad weather fell upon the crops, so that they were seldom harvested sweet and good. Poor food puts a poor heart in a horse, so our ploughing team, Kitty and Boxer, once valiant colts like Prince, had had the fire quenched in them early.

It was "Gee Boxer," and Boxer would start. "Gee Kitty," and Kitty would start. But by that time Boxer had stopped. It is weary work ploughing like that. And all the while the real muscle of the farm was prancing about in the horse-yard, or making perpetual holiday in the horse pasture.

"This won't do. Prince must be put to work," I said.

"There, did you hear that?" expressed Kitty's ears.

"We've not a bit of ground suitable," objected old Jim from a dark corner.

"What do you mean?"

"There want to be a bit of real rough ground to take him on for a start."

"We'll make a fallow of Spring Field: that'll be rough enough."

So Spring Field was ploughed up with infinite labour by Kitty and Boxer. "Come on," urged Kitty, "the quicker we get this ploughed, the sooner Prince will have to do his share of the work." Boxer responded, as far as in him lay.

"Now there's eight acres of good rough ground," I said.

"That's too hard; we need a rain to soften the clods," said old Jim. A good soaking rain soon came.

"To-morrow we'll start to break him in." Old Jim had nothing more to say, but looked funereal.

The next morning, when I came into the stable, old Jim still tried to look funereal. He said, "Prince has hurt his foot: he's cut it somehow, just above the hoof. Or rather I'd hardly say he's cut it," he added. "Seems more as though he's busted it open."

Together we examined the cut: it was a nasty flesh wound. Together we wondered how he did it. Probably against a corner of the water tank that stood in the yard. I was vexed and drew the obvious moral. "That's what comes of having a horse standing about doing nothing," I said. Old Jim began, "I remember a horse once. . . ." But he had lost his audience.

Spring came: the busy season. One evening, after a hard day pulling the corn drill, Boxer was so annoyed with Prince still nursing his bad leg and asking, "What is work?" that he kicked out sideways. Unfortunately, unknown to Boxer, I was standing between him and Prince, and received the kick on my knee.

One sunny day, when larks could be heard singing above the young corn, the songs of spring were quenched by a humming, whirring, rattling noise. A lorry backed into the farmyard; then something descended from it down some planks with a still greater whirring and rattling, and entered the shed next door to the stable.

The three horses paused in eating their dinner, and in the silence that followed saw a green creature through the gap of a missing board in the partition wall—a green thing with wheels, quite silent now, quite still, with a queer, uncanny smell. Its name, written on it, was ERT 858.

All night ERT never spoke, never moved. In the morning received no food, but was given a drink which it imbibed through the top of its back; then suddenly roared and rushed out, with the new master on its back.

The three horses stood a long while in the stable, wondering. At last old Jim entered, and put, as usual, the cart harness upon Kitty. But she was back again quite soon. "Only a load of straw," she said.

The horses were given a feed at midday, but ERT did not come back for any dinner. And still the horses stood there. At about five o'clock ERT returned to its shed, and stood roaring and shaking for a minute, then coughed twice, and was silent.

No food was brought to it; it did not stamp and look round, as Prince did, as soon as he heard the latch of the corn-bin lifted. "ERT doesn't even sweat," said Boxer. The horses were let out into the horse-yard for the night to eat hay. ERT never moved, never spoke: did not lie down, nor rub against the door.

The next day the same thing happened. The horses fed and stood: ERT roared and rushed out.

"This is all right," said Boxer, and shifted from one leg to another. "That green animal seems to like work."

Old Jim brushed them down occasionally, and cleaned out the stable. One morning he even began brushing Boxer's hooves.

Boxer glanced down at his foreleg. "Look, he's polished it. I say, this *is* all right."

"I don't like it," Kitty answered. "The last time hooves were blacked in this establishment, they were my mother's, and when she went out of that door she never came back again. No, I don't like it." She shook herself violently.

"Sign of rain," I said to old Jim light-heartedly. Old Jim said nothing, had no old story.

Boxer looked round at him. "Why, the old man's got black polished hooves, too."

"Polished hooves aren't natural on this farm, on beast or man, and I don't like it," Kitty shook herself again.

Presently Boxer was led out, admiring himself.

"Without harness, as I guessed," Kitty observed.

"You *are* cheerful this morning," Prince said. "It used to be work that made you sigh; now it's no work."

They waited and waited. ERT came back. But not Boxer.

"He had a number painted on his backside," whispered the black-and-white cat who was born in the manger, just under Boxer's nose, and had ever since been friendly.

"So has ERT," said Prince. "It must be the fashion."

"ERT's not gone to work this morning," they observed.

"Mr. Prince, now you look out," cried puss, and darted off after a mouse as old Jim and I entered the stable.

"What's this they've put in my mouth. I can bite it, but I can't swallow it. I don't like this thing round my neck, and all this jingling-jangling whenever I move."

"You'll get used to it," chuckled Kitty.

A bridle and harness look strange on a colt at first. The blinkers seem to quench his natural fire. "Now, at last," I said to myself, as we led Prince out. I had waited months for this day, though it was to be anything but a holiday. It was July now, and I had planned to break him in in April. First it had been the state of the ground, then it had been his bad foot, now old Jim was objecting it was the wrong time of the year—too hot, too many flies—hoping perhaps to lead round to the spring again, and "ground too hard." But I was determined on it, however torrid, however many flies. This horse should cheat me and the farm no longer. Jim, as he brought Boxer's old collar to put upon Prince, reminded me of an undertaker's mute handing a wreath. He looked so lugubrious I almost had to laugh, until I reflected that this man was a horsekeeper, a ploughman by profession from his youth up, by choice and by heredity. Yet I must break *him* in to the idea of taming this colt. I realized that my relief at leading out my Prince upon the deep fallow earth of Spring Field, was that my worst fight was over, the mental battle against a will straddled four-square and resistant. From April to July, how often had I returned to the attack; and oh, the veering away into stories of other horses, past days and people. Anything but this day and this horse.

Always, on the land, before matter is conquered, mind must be directed, charged, infused. Emotion there is in plenty: contact with the land generates it. *That* is the unbroken colt of every day. The horse is the very visible and tangible embodiment of what one wrestles with daily.

So we took him upon the fallow field: the soil was deep and loamy, because I had harrowed it after a shower, breaking down the clods—too soon for the good of the fallow, but for the sake of breaking the colt. Prince sank his hooves in it; he plunged and began to run (as he thought) away. His surprise at being pulled up sharp by that thing in his mouth was complete. Jim and I had each a firm hold of an end of new plough-line; sometimes Prince veered towards me, and Jim pulled him up; sometimes towards Jim, and I did. Sometimes it was as much as both of us could do to hold him: we had to run, and crouch, and run again.

Soon Prince was covered with a white lather, as though he had been dipped in the wash-tub. The sweat ran down our faces, and I could feel it trickling down my chest and back.

D

Yet the exercise was hardly more violent, I guessed, than that of our peasant ancestors in their country dances.

Prince reared up, became heraldic, rampant, puissant. He was the great war-horse of old England. He tried to jump out of the harness of toil back into the age of tilt-yard and spear and panoply. His hooves were hammers of death to any that might be under; but muffled by the deep fallow they fell silently. It looked like Prince's country dance.

How great a part this lifting of the foot played in old English life: leaping, stamping—the prance of power. The unbroken spirit of earth-bound men, trying to jump out of their harness of toil.

But now all that sweat of constraining the pounding hoof is done in the mind, and the hands hold only measuring instruments. We have made of the leaping leg the piston-rod, and its action is the piston-stroke, imprisoned in the iron cylinder of the tractor.

We have done with the wasteful exuberance of Prince pounding the air, us hanging on to him; muscle *versus* muscle. (We are onlookers now at sport.) We have done with the country dance.

Prince, too, in a while had done. He reared no more; he leaped no more, nor ran, nor walked, but stood nonplussed. His flanks heaved: he had run himself to a standstill. He stood bewildered. The first stage was over.

We let him stand like that for awhile, then chirruped at him to proceed. He moved only his ears. We twitched the reins and prodded him. In a minute he started to go forward at a quiet, measured pace. It was his first movement in obedience to human command.

Presently we unhooked the plough-traces from where they were looped up to the hames, and hooked them to a whipple-tree attached by a chain to an old railway sleeper. This was the second stage in his education.

He felt for the first time the load against his shoulders when he pulled. He started backwards, sideways, and found himself caught in the chains. Then followed a to-do, out of which he tried to jump again; but he did not leap far with a railway sleeper for partner. Once more he started forward quietly, dragging the sleeper, until the noise the sleeper made scraping over the earth frightened him, and he tried to run away from it. We hung on until the cord bit into our flesh, and presently he realized that the noise was with him all the time, like the weight against his shoulders.

And hanging on to him we two men became one man and one force. It was with us as it had been with the first men who had sought to harness a power greater than their own to the task of breaking the earth. It was not that they were stronger than the horse they tried to tame, but that they were more cunning. Man had the power of mind, and so gained the mastery. But it is not with muscle as with mechanism: conquer the lightning once and you have it harnessed—in electricity—for ever, by a formula. But every time you wish to harness horse-power of flesh and bone you must re-enact the ancient struggle. Old Jim and I were the first men united by an idea, and Prince was the first horse to be broken to it. Our hands were marked by the pattern of the plough-cord white across our flesh. Yes, the struggle with brute nature achieves a kinship between man and man, that they could not themselves achieve. Men must be united *against* something: and Chaos is the grandest enemy—the first and the last. In a horse or in a world gone wild with power.

Mind has the ultimate mastery. And who rules mind? That is, for mind, a choice.

Old Jim was in his element. Strangely, after the first delay and difficulty of bringing him to the point of leading out Prince upon Spring Field, he was now all for making a thorough job of it. His small stature confronted the great horse with the assurance of a toreador: he allowed Prince to wind himself up in the chains by making him turn sharply, crying out, "There, that's just what I wanted you to do: now you know what plough-traces feel like." And Prince would stagger and try to kick, and almost sit down. Then we disentangled him, old Jim venturing daringly near his hind feet to do so, with only a "Woa" for protection. I marvelled at this man, for months evading, deferring the day; preferring for work-mate the slow, meek Kitty. Now he was thoroughly roused out of himself, and wild horses were his pleasure.

"Give me that other rein. Now, gee up, Prince." Leaping upon the log, he drove the horse himself: he stood balanced upon the swaying, lurching thing, speeding over the fallow. It became a sport, something between surf-riding and sledging, being dragged on that narrow craft over the brown waves of earth, the kind of feat for which natives of fine physique are admired. This little old toil-worn figure could balance perfectly.

Thus, after much sweat and effort, we achieved that first stage in the evolution of transport, when man first rode and a horse first pulled him. Mind was coming into its kingdom, and aching muscle obtained relief.

We led Prince back to the stable, blown and drooping. Kitty trotted across the yard to meet him, and made a playful bite at his neck. Prince did not respond. He ate his oats and chaff, and continued with his head low in the manger. Kitty cocked her ears to and fro, a high-headed, holiday Kitty. "Now, my lad, you know."

The next day, after more of the log, we hitched him to the plough beside Kitty. This was a real pull, and Kitty let him feel it, not over-exerting herself. "You've asked often enough what work is, now you've the chance to find out." Prince was all of a fluster: once or twice he reared himself into a war-horse again. But we made him lean into the collar and pull. Every time the plough was turned at the end of the furrow, he of course became entangled in the chains. He was impatient to stand, yet unwilling to go: the furrows of that ploughing were a graph of Prince's behaviour, which was erratic. Kitty became his tutor. "Now then, clumsy, don't come barging up against me: I'm supposed to be walking in this furrow." First he would push her out over the ploughed land, then pull her on to the unploughed. Prince, I think, received a lecture on ploughing manners that night in the stable.

"What a state you're in: anybody would think you'd ploughed an acre. I wish Boxer were here to see you."

"Boxer's pulling a dust-cart round the town," said the stable cat. "I've seen him. Children give him apples. Good stable; pleasant company; lots of corn and short hours: very happy. He says, 'Next time hooves are polished don't be sad.'"

So at last Prince was taught to pull the plough, and every day went out with Kitty to plough again that fallow. But harvest was soon upon us, and there was no more time for ploughing. I don't think Kitty was sorry. The breaking-in of Prince had not proved the relief for her she had expected. Previously she had ploughed with Boxer, who moved at her own rate: now she had Prince as a partner, who moved twice as fast and kept bumping against her as well. He made turning at the end of the furrow an ordeal for her. In fact she worked twice as hard since Prince had been broken in as before.

My own triumph at having Prince in harness and old Jim minded to use him was also short-lived.

It was time to cut the hay. "He's not been used to being harnessed to a pole: the jiggle of it will upset a young horse like him, and likely he'll run away and break something." The old defeatist attitude was back in Jim. I let him have his way this time, and ERT cut all the crops for me, while Kitty and Prince decorated the pasture.

It was time to cart the corn. "But that won't do to try carting it with him: the rustling of the sheaves will upset him."

The harvest could not wait, but the education of Prince to shaft-work could: nor could I risk the smashing of a wagon when every one was needed. So ERT was hitched to a wagon, Kitty to a cart, and Prince sunned himself in the pasture.

Harvest was gathered. It was time to cart the manure out upon the stubbles.

"Now," I said, "we'll put Prince between a pair of shafts."

"It would be best to start him off between the shafts of the roller."

"All right, then."

"But there want to be a real rough bit of ground, else he might get away with it." The fallow of Spring Field had already been sown with wheat. "The spring's the best time for that job," said Jim hopefully.

"That horse is going between shafts this autumn; in fact, to-day," I said. The mental fight was on again.

Once more the atmosphere of the stable was merry as a funeral bell. No one could put a more desperate pathos into the words, "Come on, then," than old Jim as he approached Prince with the horse-collar. No one could burden with more explosive pessimism the one word "Woa" than he, as he prepared to lay the cart-saddle and breechens harness on Prince's back. Prince jumped, whether at the impact of the word or the harness I don't know.

We led him out, more "clothed" than ever before, looking like a wild tribesman who has put on hat and coat. I can never suppress a feeling of shame (hardly too strong a word for it) in cluttering for the first time the clean lines of a horse with bridle, bit, blinkers and harness. Prince had grown to take the freedom of the farm as his by right. But I knew the hour had come: either now he would rule us or we should rule him.

Old Jim was quite content to have him as one would have a pet dog, or a pet lion. Old Jim, I thought bitterly, with his manifest kindly virtues, would have been an excellent keeper at the Zoo.

To put a horse into a cart for the first time is rather like experimenting with the atomic bomb—you never know when it, or he, is going off; or, in fact, what is going to happen. You do know that the descent of shafts on either side of him is going to be a shock, likewise the rumble of wheels behind him. Our method was to make Kitty draw the cart to the manure heap in the field, then lead Prince out to it.

The shafts came down over his shoulders: it is always a nice matter whether he swings his haunches aside before the shafts have caught and trapped them. Rather like the chip-chop part of Oranges and Lemons. Then to keep him still while a good heavy load of manure was loaded upon the cart. All worked at high pressure to achieve this, and by the time Prince's restlessness was becoming unmanageable he had three-quarters of a ton to drag along with him over soft earth.

Away he went, with Jim and I on either side, each holding a rein. He plunged over the ground, snorting and fuming; a wondrous engine of power. Once more he tried to jump, run, plunge into freedom.

I prayed for the steady nerve and mind of men who had gone before and achieved the mastery. Old Jim had been visited again by their spirit. The change in this man, when the encounter with horse was on, was another miracle. It expressed itself in continuous monologue to the horse. He and Prince were engaged in deep debate of mind and muscle, locked in a grip of such tense persuasion as wrings a supple withy to make a bond.

Prince soon had enough of pulling the cart as though it were a fire-engine, and dropped into a walk. From a walk into a stand. When he stood the thing behind him was silent, and the pressure on his collar was eased. So he thought the best way to forget it was to stand still in it. But we thought otherwise. The next time he moved forward it was at our command. The rest of the day he spent in carting manure. For the loading of the last load, he stood at the heap with no one at his head.

"Oh, he's *all right*," cried Jim confidently. "All he wants is use."

"We'll use him every day for everything," I decreed, and we parted for the night in that frame: the sunset sky glowed with our achievement.

I slumped down in the basket chair in the kitchen, the one whose comfort makes a long business of the taking off of muddy leggings and boots. I said, "Prince has been in a cart—he has carted muck all the afternoon."

My wife at the stove turned round. "Prince—oh, well done!" The children came in at that moment: "Children, Prince has been pulling a cart!"

They clapped their hands. "Then Prince is a real horse at last," Sylvia added. "So poor Kitty won't have to do all the work any more." We all beamed with pleasure.

Next morning, as I came out after milking, I saw old Jim and the boy and cart and horse at the stack, getting a load of straw. But the horse in that cart was not Prince, but Kitty. Old Jim saw my thoughts. "I didn't reckon that'd be safe to take him for this job—with no one to stand by him."

There was justice in this remark, but I could tell by his look that there was many a mental fight ahead.

Meanwhile ERT worked the farm. At every objection of old Jim's, at every unpreparedness of our horse's mind and frame for the seasonal task, ERT stepped—was driven, rather—into the breach. ERT cut the hay and carted it, and the corn. ERT ploughed the stubble. ERT harrowed. An iron attachment was forged, and ERT pulled the corn-drill. Yes, ERT sowed the corn, a thing never done on this farm without horses since the invention of the drill. What is more, ERT pulled both corn-drill and harrows together, so that as the corn was drilled it was harrowed in.

One might almost say, ERT worked with a will. But ERT had no will. Yet there were times, as I travelled home in the dusk, with my head full of her whining song, that I wanted to say to ERT, "Well done!" But it would have been of no use: no use either to cry, as I once heard a farmer, "Woa!" to a tractor sliding into the ditch. Tireless, soulless, and not always obedient. You come to learn that this creature, too, needs some managing; is a temptation at times to speed at the expense of thoroughness. The man who manages a tractor must manage himself. Ditches have an attraction for tractors. The first illusion is that if you turn the front wheels, the tractor will turn. On the contrary, if the state of the soil or the load is such, the tractor will continue straight on toward the ditch, do what you will.

Another illusion is that when the power is applied the tractor will automatically go. By no means. A phrase recurs in the autumnal conversations of tractor farmers: "She scrab."

Have you ever seen a beetle trying to climb out of a bath? She scrab. Likewise a tractor trying to plough ground that is sticky. When a tractor's progress ceases to be horizontal, it very quickly becomes vertical, until she rests on her belly on the cold mud like a sow; and to resolve that predicament man must resort to his first implement of husbandry, the spade.

"Poor thing," you then feel like saying to it, as to an idiot, an aberration; as it wallows, and can only wallow itself deeper into the mire. Then what powerlessness of power is summed up in the phrase, "She scrab."

The ordinary citizen has no idea how often tractors bog and ditch themselves. What desperate churning up of soil goes on.

Ah, how beautifully little of a horse touches the ground. That is our thought for November.

It was time to cart the roots. I sat milking, when old Jim came in. "We'll have both horses and carts going: it won't take us long then," I said.

Old Jim said nothing for a minute, then ventured, "Best not take *him*. He'd not make a job of backing a loaded cart round to the clamp in the mud."

"What's the matter with that horse?" I cried.

"Oh, he's *all right*, he just needs use."

"Then use him."

The first mangolds bounced into the cart with thuds, and Prince tried to bounce out of it. But we caught him and held him, and he grew used to the thuds of mangolds, even to one bouncing off his buttock occasionally. And he learned to back the cart.

One day we were backing him between the upraised shafts of the cart, ready to lower them. They were just being lowered when he swung round, and his haunch pushed aside the boy who was holding the shafts. They descended on his back with a bump. The next time we tried to back him to the shafts he remembered that bump, and swung first to one side, then to the other; would not stand straight between them. We tried for an hour, then had to tie his head to a post, and draw the cart to him. That became the only way to get him between shafts. It was a set-back. It meant also that two people were needed if he was to be used between shafts. In meant, in practice, that old Jim reverted to Kitty.

I sent Prince to the blacksmith to be shod. Prince at the blacksmith's "created wonderful," and so objected to shoeing that in the end he sat down. The blacksmith soon had him up again though. Prince tried all his tricks, and time and time again the blacksmith's box of nails and tools were scattered by one of his hooves. It cost me quite a lot, that shoeing.

The cry was, "He wants work, he's not had enough work."

When you have a fine horse, exuberant and powerful, the farm tends to be run to provide exercise for the horse. In planning the day I found myself saying, "Prince must go to work." But ERT had done most of the ploughing. Well, then he must cart. I kept someone back to help put him between shafts, to help take him out. Jobs which one man could have done with Kitty I sent two to do with Prince. At last I began to feel, "He's becoming a tame horse."

I sent the boy one day to cart manure with him alone. Prince returned at full gallop through two field gates without the boy. I shall not forget the sight of him charging towards me down the home meadow nor the crash with which he and the cart hit the gate. By a miracle neither he nor the cart were hurt. I caught him there and held him until he ceased to pample with his feet, and stood still.

As I led him to the stable I thought, "I could sell this horse for seventy guineas, and with Kitty and ERT do all the work of this farm without trouble. Surely power on the farm—horse and tractor—should be a means and not an end."

That would be one way out. But it would be the wrong way. It would mean letting my mind succumb to old-Jim-mentality: it would mean failure to govern the horse's power, which would mean being governed by piston-power, in having to set ERT to do things when "she scrab."

Prince is a challenge. He may be Prince, but he shall not be king. I shall have mastered this farm only when I have mastered that horse.

Wold Shep

By A. G. STREET

HE woke up at five a.m. He had done this every morning for almost as long as he could remember, winter and summer, Sundays and weekdays; and had even forced himself to obey the new-fangled single and double summertime, that he hated and despised as something immoral. But if his sheep, or rather his master's sheep, had to be tended according to the altered clock, he, their shepherd, must fit his life to match theirs.

He lay quiet for a few moments in the dark, dark because the date was mid-August, 1945, which meant that the true time was a full hour earlier. He stretched himself in the double-bed, and once again thought of the wife who had lain there by his side until she died five years before.

A light flashed for a moment across the low window of his bedroom, and he listened to the noise of a car's passing.

"H'm!" he grunted. "Young Bob Allard be up to time 'smornin'. Ay, milk be all the thing nowadays. They do haul dairy volk to work in a moty, but shepherds still got to walk. Zo I maun git up."

He dressed, came downstairs, lit the lamp and kitchen fire, and put the kettle on. Maria Bates, a decent widow woman, came in every day to make his bed, clean the cottage, and prepare a hot meal ready for when he returned home in the evening at five-thirty. But the rest of his housekeeping he did for himself.

It was probably because he lived alone in this fashion that the inhabitants of Sedgebury Wallop had almost forgotten his rightful name, Walter Toomer, and usually spoke both of him and even to him as "Wold Shep." Yet he wasn't so very old. Only sixty-eight and upright as a bolt; and he could still carry a niche of hurdles on his back across muddy folds a deal better than many a young man. Moreover, like most shepherds, he had dignity. But when a man lived alone, did for himself, spent most of his waking hours up in field with his flock, and obviously did not think that modern youth was marvellous, he seemed much older than sixty-eight. Indeed, to most of his neighbours he seemed as old and as crabbed as Methuselah.

Outside the village was very quiet. Here and there a lighted window decorated the silent street; but this was the only sign of human activity, for the cows were being milked a mile away in the fields by a mechanical outdoor outfit.

But the birds had been awake a long time before. The first to herald the dawn were the cocks amongst the poultry. Then, a full hour before sunrise, the skylark arose, mounted high in the night sky, and there sang his song amongst the stars by the light of a paling moon. Shortly afterwards all the birds were busy with their dawn chorus. Pigeons cooed, partridges buzzed, snipe drummed far away from their home in the meadows by the chalk stream, and sparrows and starlings chattered and gurgled.

Dawn came first of all to the top of the downland ridge, high above the village. The night sky overhead lightened to egg-shell blue, and a pinkish smoke appeared on the eastern horizon. Light came before the sun, showing the tops of the elms that guarded the village like dark blobs in a huge bowl of soapsuds, for the valley was still shrouded in mist. Two hares slowly lolloped across the short turf, and turned sharply uphill when they heard the put-put of the milking machine engine in the valley below. Soon after this a thin red crescent rose above the eastern horizon, and a fiery ball mounted rapidly until the sun suddenly shone out in all his glory, proceeded to lick up the mist below him, and yet another hot harvest day began.

Soon after six-thirty the village woke up properly. Men whose work lay some miles distant set out on bicycles, both motor and push. Just short of seven the farm-workers made their way towards the farm-buildings, where they received their orders from the farmer; and a few minutes after seven the village was a hive of noisy activity, up-to-date mechanized farming sending tractors and cars and lorries buzzing all over the place.

But Wold Shep was not amongst those who went up to the farm for orders. He was in full charge of his department, planning his work according to his own notions of what was best for his flock. Day labourers, carters, and tractor drivers had to be told what to do each day, but stockmen, especially a head shepherd, knew what to do, and were above all orders.

So Wold Shep finished his breakfast, filled his nammett basket, douted his fire, fed his pig, and did not set out for work until a quarter past seven.

"Plenty early enough, too," he muttered, as he locked the cottage door, and put the key under a brick by the side of the porch. "This yer dratted daylight savin' 'ave upset everythin'."

He unchained his two dogs, put his basket over his shoulder, and began a slow purposeful plod along the village street, and then up a steep rutty farm road towards the fold.

Most of the sheep were lying down when he arrived, the ewes in one fold and their lambs in another. He inspected both lots quietly, to make sure the night had brought no troubles, and then plodded over the folded ground to the shepherd's house on wheels. He unlocked this, and stowed his basket inside. Then he chained up the young dog under the house, and walked over to the cake troughs. He had turned these upside-down yesterday after feeding the lambs, in order to prevent rain wetting them during the night. The old dog sat and scratched while his master set the troughs right way up for feeding. He then returned to the house, the dog following him, clambered up the three steps and disappeared inside. Half a minute later he came out with a bag of food on his shoulder.

"An' a main small bag 'tis, Rover," he said to the dog. "But all as we kin git cause o' the war. Thic 'Itler 'ave a lot to answer for. They do say as he'm dead, but I 'low death wur a tarble deal too good fur 'im."

Having put the food in the troughs, he let out the lambs from their night fold, and stood watching them as they fed eagerly.

"Not much, me dears, is it?" he said aloud. "But you be doin' vairish. I'low you wun't shame the Guvner come Wilton Vair."

"Ay, jist as I 'lowed," he continued. "Two er dree wi'

maggots. Good 'arvest weather do mean more work for shepherds. Well, I'll zee to they immejit, fur thiccy rape an' turnips
be main naish, zo 'twun't 'urt fur 'em to wait awhile fur their
green grub. G'ie the sun time to lick up zum o' the dew. Lucky
as I got thic empty vold. Hey, Roger, git away roun' 'em."

The dog helped him drive the lambs into a bare fold, and
there to hold them up in a corner, so that his master could
catch with his crook the ones afflicted with fly blows. Each
sufferer was held in turn between the shepherd's knees, and its
rump dressed with a liquid that brought the maggots towering
out.

"That's the lot, I 'low. Come away, Rover. We'll have 'em
bide where they be till atter lunch, an' shift the ewes."

The dog stood alert, keeping the hungry ewes back, until
the shepherd had removed three hurdles from one side of their
night fold. At the word of command he came to heel, and
permitted the ewes to scamper quickly into the fold the lambs
had occupied the day before. In it there seemed to be only a
few dirty leaves, some stumps of rape, and one or two shells of
turnips; but the August procedure was for the fatting lambs to
have the first go at the crop, and for the mothers to clear up
what they left. This meant that the rape and turnip field was
cleared as bare as a badger, all that remained of the crop behind
the ewes being faint lines of rape stumps chewed close to the
ground, and sheeps' droppings showing as brown chestnuts on
the white chalky soil. For the ewes ate everything edible, even
the weeds.

"Now, I 'low as the lambs kin 'ave a bite, Rover. The sun
bin right strong quite a piece."

He let the lambs into a new fold of greenstuff, and stood
watching them for a moment or two, the only sound being the
quick eager nib-nib-nib of their jaws as they tore at the succulent
leaves.

"An' now we'll 'ave a lunch."

The shepherd sat in the sunshine on the floor of the house
with his feet on the second step. Breakfast for him was not a
meal, but merely a dew bit and a cup of strong tea; but lunch
at nine-thirty or thereabouts was a good feed of bread and cold
boiled bacon. This was eaten slowly and tidily, while the dog
crouched below, and received the bacon rind and a few scraps
of bread. Lunch finished, the shepherd lighted his pipe, and

then dragged out a watch from the recesses of his long-sleeved corduroy waistcoat.

"Ten minutes short o' ten. Well, they've 'ad twenty minutes, Rover. Long enough, I 'low, zo we'll git 'em back fur a spell. I do 'ate blowed sheep."

From then until noon the shepherd carried hurdles forward from the used folds, and pitched them into a new one ready for the lambs to occupy on the morrow, the only break in this work being to let the lambs back into their fold, after they had been out of it for safety's sake for perhaps an hour. By this time the sun had dried off the dew, making the greenstuff less likely to blow any of them.

About eleven o'clock, as he slid the last heavy niche of hurdles from his back, he noticed a car coming across the field towards the fold.

"Yer's the Guvner," he muttered. "Lord, 'ow he do buzz about in thic car durin' 'arvest-time. Like a bumble bee. Still, 'ee do varm."

He walked out of the root field and met his employer as the car pulled up near the house. The two men had been together for forty years, and so their conversation as they inspected the sheep was not that of employer and employed, but of two equals in farming knowledge, in fact almost a case of deep calling to deep.

"Mornin' Shep. Everything all right?"

"Ay, jist a vew maggoty ones. But I've a tackled 'em. Now look, do 'ee want I 'arvestin' this evenin'?"

"Unless you've something special on, I do. We're jammed forty ways, and this weather won't last for ever."

"True enough. Well, I wur gwaine to round-tail zum o' they lambs. But I kin put that off to another night, if you be stuck. What do 'ee want I to do? 'Elp load sacks?"

"No, Shep. Leave that to the younger chaps. There's a patch of barley badly down in the pikked corner of the Forty Acre. Neither combine nor binder'll make any sort of hackle at it, so I wondered if you could manage to chip it off wi' your scythe. 'Taint' much, say forty rod."

"Well—I low—as I could—in the manner o' speaken. But I tell 'ee one thing, maister. Whenever you got some ticklish job wot none o' yer machines ner none o' yer young men kin do 'tis I er some other wold man wot got to do it. An' wot's moor, I kin."

"True, shep, and I should be badly off wi'out you and the other old hands. But you and I've got to face it—modern farming is a young man's game."

"Mebbe, an' they be good chaps, the main on 'em. They do a lot as you an' I cain't, and they do know a lot as you an' I doan't, but I do know zummat else. That there's a limb ov a lot as they don't know, neet you."

"Such as, shep?"

"That you bin pullin' the groun' to feed the town during the war. Nothin' but right. But now do 'ee know enough to get busy puttin' back wot you've a took out? Ef you don't, the land'll suffer, which bain't good varmin'."

"All right, shep, we'll see to it."

"Mind you do, an' mind summat else. My sheep and hurdles got to be shifted, day atter to-morrer. I shall want a man, a tractor, an' a wagon all day, an' I bain't gwaine to be put off fur nothin', zee?"

"All right, you shan't. Blast this daylight saving. Dinner-time afore we can get along. But I'm driving everything to get finished while this weather lasts. That's the trouble with combining. You can't do it until the stuff's dead ripe. If I'd been on the old-fashioned plan with binders, I'd have had everything cut by now."

"Wot of it? You'd mebbe had a lot o' sheaves out in field wet through to the bond. Naw, I finds no vault wi' yer combine. Thic fashion you don't cut nothin' till you gets it safe. 'Tis yourn from the word go, like. If rain do come, the rest o' the corn's stood up an' soon dries. No, maister, you be right to move wi' the times."

"Maybe you'm right, but I was never one to wait for things. I like to shove 'em at my own pace. But it'll be several days before I can get at the barley in Pike's Piece."

"Which I do know jist as well as you do. But, maister, thease waitin' fur corn to get ripe bain't zo much atter all. Lookeezee, you sowed thic barley last March. 'Tis now August. You've a left it to the Almighty fur about six months. Thee bide patient, an' let un 'ave it they dree moor days. Do 'ee good and the barley good, too."

"I reckon you've the rights of it, shep. But I mustn't wait here any longer, or I shall be late fetching those volunteers."

Wold Shep watched his employer drive away, and then went

back to his work, finishing his hurdle pitching by twelve o'clock. During the next hour he ate his dinner, smoked a pipe, and then slept for perhaps twenty minutes as soundly as a child, asprawl his overcoat on the shady side of the house, for by this time the sun was full strong overhead.

At one o'clock he awoke, locked up the house, and loosed the young dog, which gambolled frantically around him. Then he inspected the lambs once more, and, finding all was well with them, proceeded to let out the ewes. At this the young dog barked in gleeful expectation of work to follow; but a command from his master brought him to heel with his tail down in dejection.

"No, Rough, you be too light-headed fur thease capers. Thee an' I'll lead, an' Rover, mind thee work, oot?"

Flock, shepherd, and dogs moved slowly across the field in the commanded formation, presenting a truly biblical picture, save that the shepherd was minus a beard; and then took the road up the hill towards the downs. There the sheep busily grazed, the dogs sat by their master waiting for orders, while he leaned on his crook and surveyed the valley fields far below. He had known the farm in all winds and weathers for forty years, so it was small wonder that the present scene of furious harvesting and modern farming moved him to soliloquize aloud.

"H'm, Bob Allard 'ave turned 'is cows into Long Croft. Not aforetime, I 'low, for Folly Ground were bare two days back. Still, Bob wur lucky to save that as grass, for thease war 'ave ploughed up the main of his grazin'. Wonder how he do like that caper? No bettern I did when they took it from the sheep to make a cow pasture of it, I reckon. Ah well, jist afore the war cows were all the go. Then the war ordered corn. An' soon they says as 'ow peace'll mean more cows than ever. Hey, Rough, git away round 'em."

The young dog turned the sheep away from the edge of a field of corn, while the older one viewed his methods from the end of the chain held in his master's hand. When Rough returned to heel the shepherd resumed his musings.

"Ah, there's Fred Trowbridge on wi' thic crawler. Jist like a tank, 'ee be. Still, 'ee do do a good job. Don't squeeze the groun' like they iron-wheeled fakeranners. 'Course in the last war the tractor ploughin' wur scandalous, jist cut an' cover, as you mid say. But I'll gi'e the young chaps their due thease time, the main on 'em do plough wi' a tractor as well as the carters do wi' 'osses. Yes, I'd ha' done better to ha' took up wi' 'chinery stead o' sheep.

"But I dunno. You cain't git fond o' a tractor, neet talk to 'im for 'ee do make sich an infernal clatter. An' I do love sheep. But young chaps be no good at 'andwork, neet 'ard work. But they kin play wi' machinery. Jist look at Bill Simmons on thic combine. I low as 'ee'll vinish thic vield this evenin'. 'Ee done 150 sacks atter dinner one day last week. Mazin'.

"Glad the Guvnor got thic pick-up baler to work close behind him. I don't like to see straw left about to git wet. An' I do thoroughly approve o' thic baler. Loose straw an' hay be out o' date nowadays. They young chaps be all right drivin' a machine to make bales, but zee 'em tryin' to load up some loose stuff on a windy day. That do downscramble 'em proper. On'y men as kin do thic job be the likes o' me, wold age pensioners. An' as we be dyin' out, there got to be a machine to tie the stuff up in tidy parcels for the young uns.

"Ees, I do approve thic baler. Bales be terrible handy for haulin' out to feed in winter time. An' I do approve thic outdoor milker, too—but I ouldn' let on to Bob neet anybody as I do. But I've watched thic outfit the last vew years, and there's no mistake about it, he do git milk an' he do improve the grass grounds. But there, 'tis jist copyin' I, atter all. I do vold me sheep, and Bob Allard do vold his cows. Reuben do do the same wi' they outdoor pigs, an' Miss Dorothy be on the same caper wi' 'er poultry. 'Tis all voldin' nowadays, which be right. You cain't varmer thic chalk land wi'out voldin' stock on it.

"Ah well, one day's time twer all sheep yerabouts, an' the shepherd wur king o' the varm. Now 'tis all corn an' potatoes, an' cows an' pigs an' poultry. I 'low I be lucky to 'ave a vew sheep. An' when we wold uns be gone, I 'low the sheep'll go too. Les 'tis grass sheep. I hates they. But the young chaps wun't niver take to a hurdled flock.

"They wun't a'blieve. Too much work about thic caper. They young uns don't like work, neet back ache. They be sittin' downers.

"Still, tidn' fur I to sneer at 'em. They done a good job in the war. Job as I couldn'a done. They flyers now. Coorse, they wur

E

sittin' down at that, but all the same I'd a zight sooner be pitchin' hurdles on me veet.

"Naw. 'Tain't no good to grouse. Times do change and men must change wi' 'em. The land do bide put, an' our job's jist same as always—to make it feed the volk. All's 'tis we do use different tools.

"But I do often wonder 'ow long thease light land kin grow good crops wi'out sheep. 'Tis amazin' wot it 'ave done durin' the war. Guvner do say 'tis because o' the artificial out of a bag. I do say 'tis 'cause o' my sheep all the years afore. There, I low we be both right, an' 'tis some an' some. Rough, mind thee work, oot?

"I spose I wur wrong to take to the sheep when I wur a boy, but it cain't be altered now. I started wi' sheep at vourteen, an' I've worked wi' 'em seven days a wik ever since, so 'tis nearly time I retired. I got the old age pension, but that idn much. Still, I ain't worked fifty-vour years an five months to the day wi' sheep an' haven't got a shillin' or two. But I maun soon gie up, fur me wold legs won't stand it to keep on much longer, poor wold legs.

"Howsomever, they maun carry I a bit varther. Hey, Rover, Rough, git 'em up together."

In this manner the shepherd thought aloud while the sheep grazed until the position of the sun checked by his watch, or the other way about, told him that it was four o'clock, and time to be moving. Back went the cavalcade to the root field; the ewes were shut in their fold; the lambs were inspected once again; the shepherd's house was locked up, and down the hill plodded Wold Shep and his dogs.

At six o'clock with a good meal inside him, he took his scythe and trudged away to the Forty Acre. There he mowed the pikked corner of barley, and also trimmed the headland under some trees, the branches of which hung so low that they had forced the combine to miss almost a full swath. This done he returned to his cottage to feed his pig and his dogs, and also to clean up a trifle. Nine o'clock found him entering the Bell Inn, where he ordered his evening pint, and sat quietly in a corner smoking his pipe, and listening to the talk around him.

For several years this had been confined mainly to two subjects, war news and modern farming methods; but to-night a new one had taken pride of place. This was the result of the recent election; which, according to some of the company present, would mean higher wages, shorter hours, and in fact little need to do any work at all. At least all the talkers seemed to think so. What the men who sat silent thought about it all nobody knew. In Wold Shep's opinion the men who talked the loudest were the ones who liked work the least.

Sid Musselwhite was the leader of the no-work-and-all-play group, but then he was always a blow-guts, all wind and precious little else worth while.

"When the Guvner be about butter 'ouldn' melt in Sid's mouth," muttered Wold Shep to the bottom of his pint pot. "But at thease minnit I 'low as cheese ouldn' choke 'im."

"Yes, chaps," Sid declaimed. "I'll tell 'ee wot'll 'appen. Now we got a Labour Government we shall be able to start when we likes, knock off when we likes and charge wot we likes. An' the varmers'll ha' to pay it. Five poun' a wik ordinary time, five poun' a yacre fur hoein' roots, five poun' a 'undred fur makin' thatch, an' five poun' . . ."

"A hour fur drinkin' beer," chimed in Bill Simmons the combine-harvester driver, amidst general laughter. "Sid, thee bist five poun' crazy."

"Oh, be I? Thee's gettin' too big fur thee boots. Jist cause thee's drive thic combine, thee's think nobody else do matter on a varm. Let's ask a fair man, who ain't combine crazy. Wold Shep now. What's thee think about it, Shep?"

Wold Shep was making his way to the street door, but at this remark he turned and faced the company.

"Wot do I think, Sid? Jist this. That atter a bit 'twill be jist the zame as it allus wur, an' should be. Work er want, an' thee't want. Good night, all."

"So now you knows," chimed in the landlord. "Time, gennelmen, please."

Portrait of a Dalesman

By Harry J. Scott

Tom Merlin is an outstanding dalesman, even in that Dale
country of the North where the hard grim fells mould gaunt
unflinching men and women, who wrest from the hills a liveli-
hood that is at all times sparse and who have accepted as their
heritage long spells of bitter years which have tested their
endurance and steeled them to solitude. History has been made
by the shape of the Pennines, and life is nowhere more its
naked invincible self than on these high lands of limestone
crags and peat bogs where mere existence calls up a splendid
hardihood. Long ages ago strong men surged from beyond the
Border over these lands, ravishing, harrying and plundering
livestock, while others came from the Baltic lands to take up
temporary possession. The tides swept back, but they left their
legacy in a few hardy souls whose strain can still be traced in
the physical characteristics of those who dwell to-day in the
villages and hamlets of the Dales.

    Winter is the testing time that makes or breaks men. Tom
Merlin can recall how when he was a stripling there was a

frost which lasted from November to May without relaxing. Sheep perished in hundreds. Lambs followed the shepherds in forlorn groups and died as they bleated after men who were powerless to help them. Then hay and straw had to be brought by horse-carrier from the south, a ruinous business when flocks were dying and even humans found it hard to get sufficient food to keep alive. He can remember how it was told that nearly a thousand sheep had been gathered together from one fell and in a short time fewer than two hundred remained.

Tom was brought up at one of those isolated farmsteads which, squat and solid, snuggle into the deeply-cut valleys that run up into the high fells. Ridged and rocky hills encompassed it on three sides, but the shelter they gave also shut out the sun for many weeks together during winter. His father gained a hard and meagre living from his sheep which roamed the fells around and Tom, after a brief spell at the mid-dale school three miles away, accepted as natural what is the lot of Dales youth to this day, an abrupt end of lessons and his initiation to farm work.

Then came the blow that brought Tom to man's estate almost before he had closed his school primer. It was in the mid-November that followed his thirteenth birthday when a deep swirling mist blotted out both sight and sound and a candle was necessary in the farmhouse kitchen at midday.

Tom had been busy about the farm. His father had taken a cart along the rough fell track intending to bring a load from an outbarn. Hours passed after the mist had swallowed up man and cart, and when early dusk began to add a denser blackness to the afternoon Tom set out along the track to help his father in.

A few hundred yards along the stony road he found him lying in an unnatural huddled way across the track, the cart with one splintered broken wheel tipped half over on the mist-soaked grassy bank and the horse tangled with much struggling in its harness, but still tethered to its unmovable load.

Tom was awestruck for a moment, and shivered as he saw a dark stain on his father's forehead.

"What's happened to thee, Dad?" he asked, as he bent down to the crumpled figure.

"Is that thee, Tom Boy?" murmured his father. "Ah'm glad thee's come to get us home."

It says much for Tom's native quickness of wit that was so belied by his normal slowness of manner that he summed up the grim situation in a way that outpaced his years. It was plain to him that he could not get the injured man back unaided. Slipping his coat under his father's head, he disentangled the horse from its traces and hurried the frightened creature in a stumbling gallop back to the farm.

His mother hurried to the door at the unusual sound in the yard.

"What's amiss, Tom?"

"Father's liggin on t'fell. He's tummelled out o' t'cart and can't stir. He's badly."

"Wheer is he? Ah mun go tiv 'im. We mun bring 'im home."

"Aye, mother. But we needs must carry 'im. He's past walking."

"But how can thee and me carry 'im down t'fell?"

"There's t'sled. I brought Jess back so as we could tak it."

So on a heap of heather and bracken piled on to the sled which they used to carry down the hay and bedding from the fell intakes they brought the dying man home to the farmstead.

To his father the lad had always been "Tom Boy," and it was to "Tom Boy" he whispered in his last spell of consciousness.

"Thou must tak over now, Tom Boy. T' farm, t'sheep and all t'rest depend on thee. Thou mun look after 'em for thi mother's sake."

"Aye, Dad," he said. "I'll try."

They were desperate uphill years that followed, but with the help of a hired man from the dale at haytime and sheep-clipping, Tom and his mother kept the farm going through the long round of immemorial tasks that begin with lambing and end with the dipping of the sheep.

And as Tom grew up in the dale and took his place among the older farmers the name his father gave him stuck. Incongruous though it was as applied to the tall lean figure with almost jet black hair, deep tanned skin, and heavy eyebrows, "Tom Boy" was his by-name down the whole length of the dale. There was only one aspect of him to which it might appropriately be applied, and that was as odd as his title. As a boy Tom had acquired a battered tin whistle, and on fine days on the fell tops he would practise a few simple tunes for hours to an audience of curious but bewildered sheep and an occasional startled grouse. Mostly they were hymn tunes and a nursery rhyme or two he had picked up at school, but if his repertoire was small it gave him a quiet delight.

Even after he had left school and had taken over the farm he still carried the battered whistle in his inside pocket and would sometimes stop for a moment on a limestone crag or against a dry stone wall and pipe out a reedy tune for his own enjoyment. That was his only concession to anything that might be called Tom Boyish. For the rest he was steel hard, tanned by all weathers, and never relaxing in the perpetual battle against storm and wind, snow blizzard and driving rain, those timeless untiring enemies of every upland farmer. He was not ambitious and therefore was not bitter against his lot.

Often he would climb to the crags above the farm and look down the dale to Slapestones, where he could see the vast and rambling establishment of the Worsleys, who were not only farmers but horse-breeders and were wealthy beyond the dreams of most dalesfolk. They owned horses and cattle and sheep and employed many men, and were acknowledged leaders in dales affairs. Beyond, where the dale broadened to the river meadows, were sleek, comfortable farms where life was comparatively easy and existence was generous. But they had no magnetic pull for Tom. He knew of their pleasant lot but was not envious. He steered clear of major disasters and lived down losses and ill-spells alike. His silent and lonely habit of life came naturally to him and became more ingrained after the death of his mother. He was naturally austere by temperament and might almost have been called monkish as he continued to live alone at the isolated farm.

There were offers made to him to buy over his farm and to give him a more comfortable life lower down the dale. If he had wished he could probably have done well in easier country. He preferred his fell farm.

"I'm a dalesman," he always said. "And a sheep man. I reckon I'm reet as I am."

In his limited dealings with the rest of the dale he was well-liked. As is accepted among men who have to struggle for a limited recompense for their labours he was one with them in driving a hard bargain. He would batter a man down almost meanly for a few pence, yet be generous in honouring his share of the bargain. It was said that he bargained for half an hour with the shopkeeper at the Winburn stores over the price of a pair of boots, and finally got them at his own figure—though the shrewd shopman had doubtless wisely prepared for this beforehand by marking up his commodities. Women, who notice little things like this more than men, remarked about a curious old-world courtesy that was his and, more surprisingly, that there was in his eyes not hardness such as you might expect from one who spent his days up on those bleak wild fells, but a sort of wistfulness.

Tom Merlin, even in the sternest conflict in the market, always kept his temper. Only once was he known to lose it, at any rate, in public. That was when he found a heavy-handed lout of a labourer beating a sheep-dog with a great ash stick. It was late one market day, and the dog was tied to a pen in the cattle market. The wretched creature was half strangled in its efforts to get away from its tormentor.

Tom strode over to the fellow with the ash plant.

"That'll do," he said. "Tha's done plenty to t'poor beast. Give ower now."

"Mind thi own blasted business," said the man, and brought down the ash plant again.

"Stop it, I tell thee," said Tom. "If tha hits that dog again I'll kill thee."

It was unfortunate for the man that he ignored the threat, though fortunate that the onlookers dragged Tom away after he had only hit him twice. It was several weeks before the lout with the ash plant lost the marks of Tom's anger.

"Nay, I made a gurt fooil o' missen," said Tom to himself later that day as he pulled out his tin whistle and piped himself into a better frame of mind. "Mi old Dad would a' bin capped if he'd known Tom Boy 'ud 'a lost his temper ower nobbut a dog."

When he was a little over forty and his black hair had taken upon itself a fine mist of grey, though his slow stride was no less firm, his sight no whit dulled, and his massive hands as steady as ever, Tom Merlin married. People in the dale were surprised, but the most critical of them agreed that if Tom Boy had to marry then the only possible wife for him was the one he had chosen. The pair were oddly alike physically; perhaps that is why they seemed so well matched. She was tall, lean—

almost gaunt—with the same strong nose and slightly up-curled chin. She gave the impression of great strength in repose, yet she was quicker in her movements than his slow gait. Like him she was taciturn, and it was many weeks before even the most knowledgeable of the dales folk knew that her maiden name was Mary Metcalfe, and that she was one of that great clan of Metcalfes which had spread from the high dales over all the North country.

Then they realized whence she derived that long bony face, that firm mouth and eyes like smoky steel which held you with the steady grip of a man's, and the soft rich musical voice. She had the qualities of the hill country.

They lived a very quiet and secluded life at the farm at dale head. Although she was considerably younger than her husband, Mary took to the hard life of a farmer's wife as though born to it—which indeed she was. She did a good deal of outside work with Tom, and was capable in handling the sheep and the few beasts they had. They worked all hours. Indeed, there were those in the dale who in those early days said that it was no life for a young woman, and that their relation to each other and to the world was almost inhuman. The farm seemed always to stand first.

Yet if ever there was any doubt in the dale about whether she was the right wife for Tom Merlin, Mary resolved it in that grim black winter when, still a young bride, she saved Tom from death on the snow-covered fell not a mile distant from the track where Tom so many years before had found his injured father. It happened just at the onset of the winter when, after a comparatively mild spell, a dull grey bank of cloud began to pile up from the north-east. By late afternoon a few thin snowflakes had thickened to a steady relentless fall, and overnight there came a blizzard which piled the snow high at every window and against every door. Tom had to dig his way out to get to his cows, warm in the shippon. Mary had to cut through a drift to reach her few hens in the hut on the home pasture. Field after field gleamed white down the dale, with just a wall-top showing at intervals.

"There'll be more coming," said Tom. "I mun get down those ewes from t'intake. They'd fare better near at hand. Maybe I should a'gone afore."

Mary doubted whether he would find them.

"They'll be deep under now. Perhaps they'll have found bield (shelter) beneath the crag. Why not leave 'em? Happen they'll take no harm."

But Tom wanted his sheep closer to the farm. If more blizzards were to come the sheep would follow their ancient instinct and run before it, over walls, across dykes, and into unknown country where disaster might befall them.

"I'll go now while there's still light enough to find their tracks," he said.

It was bitter, anxious work looking for sheep on a snowbound fell. No vast weight of snow had fallen yet, but it had drifted high against the walls and over the narrower gullies in the limestone. Sheep will take shelter against a wall or crag, but their shelter may become a tomb if the driving snow banks up around them, and they are "overblown." Only small discoloured gaps in the roof of their snow canopy where the heat of their bodies and their breath has found an outlet will betray their presence. A sharp eye or a keen-nosed dog may discover the traces, but a fell-top is a big haystack in which to seek a needle.

Tom felt that his ewes would still be within the walled intake —one of those rough pastures won back by hard toil from the moorland grass and heather. With a long pole and help of his dog he might find them and dig them out and then hurry them back to the comparative shelter of the farmstead.

The late warm light of a wintry sun had tinged with colour the white tops of the surrounding fells before Mary, listening for the peevish cry of sheep or the high note of her husband's whistle, began to be troubled by his absence. Tom knew the fells in winter and summer as he knew his own farmyard. He was not likely to be lost, but there were other perils which grew in her mind as the hours passed.

She had tended the animals and had made the round of the farm half a dozen times, partly to leave nothing for Tom to do after his wearying day, partly to keep herself occupied. Darkness came quickly after the sun dropped, and already there was a whining and a moaning in the chimney that foretold another wild night.

The first thick wet snowflakes were beginning to fill the air, laying a heavier blanket of silence on the still world of the hills when, from the slate-roofed porch of the farm, Mary saw a live black shadow moving swiftly along the rutted cartroad. It was too dark to distinguish more, but a clammy fear clutched her and she found herself breathing faster as she sensed the dog leap the wall as a short cut to the door. A moment later it was at her feet alternately nuzzling her dress, with its white-tipped tail waving like a flag, and then flopping down to pant from sheer exhaustion.

Mary wasted few words as she slipped an old coat over her shoulders and a scarf round her throat.

"Good lad," she said, "I reckon tha's come to say he wants me."

It was clear to her that the dog would not have come on alone if Tom had been returning. It would have been needed to keep the sheep from straying. In any case, Tom would have kept it well to heel on a night like this. Perhaps he was having diffi-culties in digging out the buried ewes. Maybe he couldn't find them all. Or could it be . . .?

She tried to banish the black visions as, with the dog close beside her, and with a flickering hurricane lamp to keep her out of the deeper snowdrifts she clambered up the steep fell track now fast becoming obliterated by the persistent fall.

When she reached the gate where the cart track led into the intake the dog ran wildly along the wall side. Twice she climbed over the gate that was already buried up to its second cross-bar, and called the animal to follow. Once it leaped on to the wall-top and barked, but it did not come to her. There was no footprint near the gate but her own, and no sound but the muffled rattle of a stream, and for a moment she felt a sudden helplessness. Then she turned to follow the dog.

She found Tom some time later at the foot of a shallow cliff, face down in the snow with one leg twisted hideously under him. Fresh snow had already begun to pile up on his back and head. His cap had fallen into a gulley and his long pole lay in two pieces projecting raggedly from a bank of snow. Mary slipped a hand into his jacket and started with a faint surprise as it touched the hard shape of his tin whistle projecting from the inside pocket. He was still warm, and she could feel the slow beating of his heart.

In the dale they still tell the story of how, in a nightmare journey that lasted many hours, Mary carried him home on her back, stopping from sheer exhaustion a dozen times on the way, stumbling herself as she frequently lost the track, floundering through drifts and into icy pools, reaching home cut and bruised and limp with the weight of her burden, and of how she got him into bed and brought him back to warmth and consciousness and then set off again down the dale road to get a doctor just as the first sleepy farm hands were stirring in the half-light of dawn. It remains an outstanding epic in the land where life is often lived at epic level.

In the weeks that followed Mary nursed her Tom Boy back to health, and her own ordeal left no mark upon her. Held bedfast with a broken leg and wrist and tormented by his bruises, Tom, she declared, was easier to manage unconscious than conscious. And she laughed at the old dale doctor when he showed a desire to talk of her part in the affair.

"It were nowt at all," she said.

"Tha'd better pipe yourself a tune," she told Tom when at last he could sit up. "It'll keep thi mind occupied like."

"A fellow can't pipe wi' one hand," he retorted, but nevertheless he managed to persuade "Pretty Polly Oliver" and "Onward Christian Soldiers" out of the bent and battered whistle.

From that time the dale began to take a new interest in the couple at the farm at the dale head. News spreads swiftly in isolated communities, and as the story went down the dale, Tom, and Mary particularly, found an unexpected warmth of feeling towards them. Those who had been most critical were loudest in their praise of the girl's bravery. Farmers at Winburn market doffed their hats to Mary, much to her secret amusement, and their wives hastened to have "a crack" and a gossip with her.

Yet Tom and his wife kept "thersells to thersells" very much as before, and the seclusion of their life at the fell farm was scarcely broken.

Some years after Tom's recovery it began to be whispered among the womenfolk that "Mary Merlin's expecting," and it was noticed that her visits to market became less frequent. Tom was chaffed a little when he did the household shopping, and sly jokes went round about "another tomboy expected, eh?" But he said little, though up on the fells he piped more often and his dog was frequently disconcerted when his master sat for long spells on a limestone crag and mournfully piped "Pop Goes the Weasel" or "Work for the Night is Coming," two of his favourite airs. If Tom enjoyed piping, his dog remained unappreciative and would howl miserably at the music until Tom in disgust sent him off out of earshot.

As the months went by Tom stuck closer to his farmstead, and at hay-time refused for the first time to give a hand to the mid-dale farmers. With the help of an Irish hay-timer he got in his own small crop and then found himself with an unwonted leisure. When he finished tending his stock he busied himself with jobs about the house for Mary until she drove him out, and then he would climb to the scars above the farm and sit whittling a stick with his penknife or piping to himself.

"Tha's acting daft, Tom," said his wife more than once. "Tha's no call to fret about me. I shall be reet enough. Thee go and give Jim Lister a hand wi' his hay."

But Tom was adamant and haunted the farmhouse and the crags about it throughout the long summer days. One evening in early September Tom had gone as usual to his high crag from where he had a view down the whole length of the dale. The bracken was already turning from green to bronze, and the young grouse were almost as big as the parent birds. Already some of the moorland curlews were moving off to the river estuaries, an early sign of the harder days to come. It had been a good summer, Tom concluded as he climbed through the rough grass to his eyrie. A good season like this did much to help through a bad winter if that was to come. Things had gone well with him, although if all went well there would soon be another mouth to feed in the Merlin family. That might come any time now, he thought. The old doctor had said only yesterday that things would be happening soon.

He stood up on the bare crag and noted, with a farmer's eye, the stock in his fields below. His sheep were scattered far over these fells, and there would be an ingathering soon for marking and dipping. He observed a low haze in the near distance.

"That'll be ower Slapestones," he murmured half aloud. "Queer, though, how it hangs theer and no wheer else. Never noticed that afore. Maybe t'Worsley's are cleanin' up wi' a bonfire. They need to. But it looks a gurt 'un, if so."

Just then a spurt of flame shot up through the haze, followed quickly by another. A pillar of smoke plumed up and wreathed over, and as it drifted away a gap revealed a stretch of blazing roof. It was clearly more than a bonfire at Worsleys.

Tom slipped his whistle, which he found still in his hand,

into his pocket and dropped quickly off the crag. He set off with a fast fellman's stride across the intervening moors between the dale head and Slapestones. It was rough, tortuous going with many hills and hollows and narrow steep ravines where the little moorland streams ran down from the watershed of the hills. Across them Tom picked his way, using sheep tracks and pony ways that he knew until he could cut across to an old bridle road where the going was easier.

As he hastened through the last home pasture which adjoined the outbuildings of the Worsley establishment he could both see and hear the flames as they roared and licked and leaped over the main block. For a moment Tom thought the whole estate was caught up in the great ocean of wickedly yellow flames, for smoke seemed to pour and heave round every building and shed, and he could feel the heat even on his perspiring face.

Half a dozen men were concentrated round the two storey block in the middle of the yard, and for the moment there was the fire's centre. They had formed themselves into a bucket line, but it was a pathetically hopeless business. Ted Worsley greeted Tom with a nod and a grimace.

"This lot's done for," he said. "But we might keep it from the rest."

A new shower of sparks shot up as a roof corner fell in and there was a scramble with a ladder to dislodge a blazing beam on the tiles of a cart-shed. A clutter of smouldering twigs from an overhanging tree drifted in through the open doors of a barn and Tom stamped them out and pushed the great doors together. He joined in the bucket chain, which moved from corner to corner of the blazing building seeking a point of vantage for their feeble efforts. Another Worsley brother was moving harness and horse gear from a smouldering heap in the yard.

Suddenly there was a cry from the elder Worsley.

"Look out, the stable's ablaze."

A long low line of stable buildings lay behind the blazing middle block. A wide yard between had afforded apparent safety, although a man had been spared to lead out the frightened horses to the paddock beyond. His task was half completed when the roof had flared up and the sun-dried timbers leaped into flames.

Ted Worsley darted through the smoke-filled yard calling to Tom as he ran.

"Quick, Tom Boy, or the horses will panic."

Already smoke was seeping along under the roof and half a dozen terrified animals whinneyed and reared and kicked wildly at their boxes. It was difficult to get near enough to release them, and time and again Tom was pressed agonizingly against a box wall by a lunging animal until he thought his ribs would crack. One great black beast snapped savagely at him in its terror, but he grabbed its mane and dragged it backwards into the yard. He remembered his father telling him to blindfold a horse that was frightened by fire, but there was no time for that. He could see a bright glow creeping nearer along the beams. He got two horses out into the yard where the stable lad grabbed them and hurried them off. As he brought out the third he looked round for Ted Worsley and was surprised to see a considerable crowd at work in the yard. A uniformed fireman was tugging a hose along.

"Hello, Tom," called out the man. "Bad do, this. Didn't know you were here. Ted Worsley's in a bad way, bin kicked in the head by one of them horses. They've sent for the doctor."

The fireman went off with his unwieldy hose and the stable lad nudged Tom.

"There's only one left," he said. "Can we get her?"

Like a tormented wild beast the remaining animal reared and dragged and stamped in an inferno of heat and smoke. Tom climbed up on to the side of its box and hung on precariously as he slipped out of his jacket. Clinging with one arm to an iron pole by the hay rack, with the other he dropped the jacket over the animal's head. It slipped off again, but he managed to grab a sleeve. At the second attempt he got it fairly over the creature's ears and eyes, and as the horse paused uncertainly the stable lad ran in and grabbed its nose. It retreated suddenly and, after a wild plunge, backed out of its box into the yard. And as it stumbled out Tom heard the metallic tinkle of his tin whistle on the stone floor.

Men patted him on the back as he staggered out through the smoke into the yard.

"Good owd Tom Boy," they cried.

"Thou's about fagged out," said the farm foreman. "There's a drink waiting for thi. Come on."

Still dazed by the smoke and heat, Tom was lead by the arm into a shed. At the door he blundered into a stumpy figure coming out.

"Steady there," said a familiar voice. "Bless me, if it isn't Tom Merlin. Wait a minute, Tom. I've some news for ye."

Tom blinked and peered hard through smoke-tortured eyes at the old doctor. Then he remembered. For an hour, two hours, it seemed like hundreds of hours, he had forgotten. He had gone up to the crag to wait, for what? Of course, his wife. It was . . ."

"Nay, Tom Boy," the old doctor was saying. "I don't know what your wife will say to ye. But ye'd best get home and see if ye like the other tomboy she's given ye. Let's hope he's more sense of responsibility than his father."

THE SPIRIT OF BRITAIN

By Kenneth Belden

The Spirit of Britain is the treasure in the citadel for which we fought. It is the glory of the victory we have won, the hope for the future we shall build.

Through long centuries we have gathered resources of heart and mind which to us are beyond price. Twice in a generation we have fought to defend them.

These riches of the spirit are hard to define. They shine through the faces of mothers and children; they are seen in the men of the mine and the men of the plough; they are poured out in the heart's blood of sacrifice on countless battlefields; and they are infinitely dear in our own homes.

In these pages we have tried to picture something of the spirit of the land we love and of the men who make her great. Never have we needed that spirit more than at this time. For though it is imperishable, it is threatened. Ideas alien to the spirit of Britain are sweeping through the minds of millions in the world today.

It is for us to sustain the spirit of our heritage and to share it with mankind. On nothing less can the nations of tomorrow be securely built. It is the sentinel of liberty, the herald of the world we long to see.

This royal throne of kings . . .

This precious stone set in a silver sea . . .

This earth, this realm . . .

Though our roots lie deep in the past, in all our rich heritage of history and beauty . . .

. . our treasure lies in things nearer the heart, in the spirit of our people.

The spirit of Britain is born and nurtured in our homes. From sound homes springs the courage and endurance of the men and women of these islands.

From the training of Britain's homes

comes our love of a job well done.

We have a deep kindliness we often try to hide.
It comes out in our love of animals. *(EVEN BETTY!)*

A nation's character can be seen in its sport.

We are blessed with a sense of humour which is always bubbling to the surface.

We like our independence.

But we value and accept team work.

Because we are a democracy, we have grown up to take responsibility in our village . . .

. . . in the government of our town . . .

. . . and of our nation.

The wealth and strength of Britain comes from her industry . . .

. . . and from the men who make industry.

Yet behind the thunder of industrial cities

s the measured life of the countryside . . .

. . . of farm and village . . .

. . . of hillside and pasture

Every Briton's heart is in the countryside,

in the quiet valleys and the silver rivers.

Our spirits lift to the line of the sun-swept downs.

From these hills and fields, these farms and factories, the nation rallied

. . . for the greatest armed conflict of all time.

And now we look together to the futu

and the nation of tomorrow.

"Let us go forward . . . as one man, a smile on our lips and our heads held high, and with God's help we shall not fail."

His Majesty the King.

The Coast of
Enchanted Wings

By J. Wentworth Day

THE low coast goes shelving off, cattle marsh fading into sea
wall, sea wall into saltings, salting to mud-flat. And then the
mud-flats melt into snaky creeks and the flat and shining sea.
It is a wide and manless land of immense landscapes and glitter
of seascapes, betwixt low uplands where great farmhouses stand
yellow-walled within their moats and girdling elms, and the sea,
distant and glittering. It is lonely of ship-smoke and empty of
sail, save the far topsail of a coasting barge or the evening
armada of the fishing fleet.

It has not changed much, this long Essex coast, in the last
three centuries. If old Nicholas van Cropenbrough and his
baggy-breeched Dutchmen who embanked and drained so
much of it when the Stuarts held their uneasy thrones were to
come back, he would find the same wide marshes, cattle-

F

dotted, humming with the far monotone of a thousand sheep. They melt luminously into the same silent sea. In the clear light, redshank still ring their carillon of bells in the sweet nesting month of May. Herds of grey curlew skirl up the creeks in the rusty days of autumn and black geese in fleets still cronk on the mud-flats and sandbars in winter. Widgeon mew like cats under the moon and porpoises thresh up the rivers on warm harvest nights as they did in the golden dusk of Carolean evenings.

There is this difference though. Down on the cattle marshes, those long prairies of rough grass which cover tens of thousands of acres, the tidal creeks and guts, the rills and pools which the Dutchmen embanked behind their high sea walls are no longer muddy channels of salt water full of scuttling crabs. To-day the deeper ones are now long snaky lagoons of brackish or fresh water, reed fringed, full of coots and pochards, of reed warblers and laughing shellduck. In summer the shallow fleets are mere tortuous depressions in the cattle marsh, dry and full of springing grasshoppers and meadow pipits. In winter they fill with flood water and peewits paddle in them, the redshank bathe delicately like dancing girls and snipe probe them for worms.

Here and there, as at Clacton and Walton, at Southend and, to a lesser degree, at Mersea, the vulgarity of the building speculator has left its shoddy mark. The rowdy holiday maker and his attendant sprites of beer and whelks have transformed those East Anglian beaches into East End offshoots. But they are well defined areas. The gregarious tripper fears solitude and loathes nature. Half a mile from him the curlew stalks the mud for worms and gulls quarrel in the quiet sunlight. And in winter, that time of fowl, the trippers go home to pub and cinema, the beach huts are shut and the bitter East wind brings the geese on windy pinions from Baltic solitudes. The fowler pulls on his long boots and takes down his long gun and East Essex is again as it was and always will be—a land of birds and drifting fogs and bitter winds and the loneliness which is near to God.

That is the time to know this lonely coast, from the foghorn haunted Thames to the wider Stour, and not in the garish months of high summer. Winter is the fowler's season. Winter and the gold-red dawns of autumn when the hares lie out on the sea-walls and foxes sleep in sea-lavender far out on the salts.

Spring is the time of nesting birds and a million baaing sheep, the blessed time of young green reeds and sea-weary birds that drop in at dawn on tired wings. That is the time of the whimbrel with their clear fluting call, whom Essex fishermen call by that lovely name, "titterel." The time of sand-pipers whistling up the dykes and the goat-eyed stone curlew, of teal in the reeds and, perhaps, the rare and lovely sight of a pair of avocets, delicate as porcelain, stepping in the shallow pools. The otter whistles in the green nights and the gaunt carrion crow builds in lonely thorn bushes far out on the marsh.

Bullocks and sheep and a hermit shepherd, far skies and an oyster smack gliding red-sailed down a creek in the flush of dawn, those are my sole companions in those young dawns of the year. It is a coast for the naturalist and the wildfowler, the man who loves the solitude of a small boat in a silent creek.

The space of immense levels and high skies. The purple and silver of mud-flat, the glitter and sheen of creeping tide, the drift of suaeda pods on summer water; and the sea-wind running like mice through summer singing grasses; the clang and whistle of wildfowl and waders; the croak of geese in the winter dawns and drift of herons at snowy eve. These are the sounds and colours of this land. A roadless land and a houseless land. Down on the marshes the only roads are still the old, green, barge roads, those raised and silent trackways which run from upland farm lanes where straw hangs on the hedges and finches scold the weasel, to the hairy sea-walls where, on the creek-edge, the black piles of an ancient and disused staithe mark where once the barges lay days and nights on end while wheat was loaded or cattle were driven aboard for transport to the mainland.

For it is a coast of islands—islands with Saxon names and Norse names like Havengore and Horsey, Wallasea and Osea and Northey. Old English and salty names like Puit—the isle of peewits—and Foulness, "the cape of birds." Rushley, the rushy isle and Potton, which was walled when Charles the First was King, and Ray Island, where the ghost of a Roman centurion walks in the full moon, and Rat Island, which speaks for itself, and Skippers, the lonely isle with its heronry, where, fifteen years ago, I found the mate of the old *Cutty Sark* living in a wooden shack hid low among thorn bushes with only the bullocks and the curlew to keep him company. Then there is New England, on which no man lives, for the tides have swallowed it as they swallowed only a few years ago the whole 600 acres of Bridgemarsh Island in the Crouch, where now only the ruined chimney of the old house sticks up forlorn above the spring tides.

Consider for a moment the history which clings about the very sound of these lovely island names. There is Canvey, which Ptolemy knew as Cnossos, and whose old inn, the Lobster Smack, still peers over the sea wall as it did when Charles Dickens chose it for the hiding place of Mr. Magwitch. But that is all that you need care about Canvey.

There is Horsey, which was Horsa's Isle, the camp amid the salt tides of that Danish river, and Havengore. Havengore since it lies up a long creek off the Thames, was clearly the haven up the Gore, which was, and still is, in Norse, a channel. Wallasea is the walled island for it was walled by the Dutch, and Osea, the Oozy isle, set amid the vast Goldhanger mud-flats with Northey, northernmost of the two.

It was on Northey that on a high day in A.D. 991 the Danes, sailing up the Blackwater in a mighty and murderous armada of raven-headed ships, shield-hung, oars threshing, conquest and the raven of Odin at the mast head, made camp. They threw up a stockade on the fields where I shoot rabbits and curlew. Their longships swung at anchor in the tides off Heybridge and Mill Beach. Their skin-clad swordsmen, girt and laced, ran about and drank under the raven's elms. Anlaf, the Dane, was their chief.

To challenge them came Brithnoth, the Saxon, Ealdorman of Essex, with the men of East Anglia and met them in that epic three-day battle which ended the dominion of the Saxon in Eastern England and began the hard thrall of the Dane. But, let we brother fenmen mark well "the men of Cambridgeshire," above them all in East Anglia, held fast and strong to the bloody uttermost.

It was on the hard, pebbly sea-road between Northey and the mainland that the three champions of England, helmed and eagle-winged, in their leathern jerkins and baldrics, held the ford against the heady, shouting Danes—Aelfhere, Macchus and Wulfstan. Let their names never be forgotten.

For three mortal days of hand-to-hand combat on the

bloodied sea-surges of that slippery island road they swung their swords and split the Danish skulls, till one by one the three English champions were hewn down, the Danes swept in and all Eastern England fell under that fierce northern bond.

So I can walk on Northey, the northern isle, and think on the Northmen who died heroically.

But why Hedge End, now a drowned isle, should be Hedge End is beyond me, for I can imagine no hedge save of suaeda bushes or maybe thorn or tamarisk which would grow on that bleak soil. Cob Holm is the isle of the great cob gulls and Packing House, that mud-bank of gold in Mersea Fleet, is named so because of the gaunt wooden packing shed for oysters which stands on its oozy shores, reared on piles, just as the Colne oysters are packed in that other great shed on Rat Island in South Geeton creek. Then there is Bramble Island, hard by Horsey in Hamford Water, where the explosive works crouch in sinister solitude between great grassy mounds, and yet another Peewit Island hard by. It, too, has gone back to the crabs and the tide. Forgotten by all save a few old fishermen is that tiny tuft of salting on Goldhanger Flats called The Wild Hills. Once, a century or more ago, it was an isle of an acre or two, thick at high tide with wild geese. To-day, the scour of the fierce Blackwater tides have left no more than a few square yards.

I have been on every one, bar two, of these Essex isles. I have shot on most of them, caught great slithering eels in their fleets, punted to the shouting geese off their lonely shores and seen the terns stoop like flashing arrows at the fish in their summer shallows. And I have ridden Robert, my old hunter, or walked in long sea boots, over most of the marshes which lie lonely between Thames and Stour and even farther to the Wash in the cold Norfolk air.

This Essex coast breeds a strange, fierce love of itself. It is a country for men who love solitude and the silence of the sea. Its own men, the fishermen and fowlers, the winklers and shepherds, the bargemen and marsh "lookers," with here and there still an ancient with gold ear-rings in his ears and still, in quiet creek-head villages, "wise women," who will charm your warts away and cure your cows, these people are a race apart. They are the authentic salt of the earth, as salty in mind, as bracing in speech as the sea-verges which nursed them. They are supreme individualists, fierce in independence, polite with nature's own courtesy and witty with that spontaneous wit which puts the townsman's thought-out, reiterated jokes to shame. For though you will often enough hear apt aphorisms, shrewd comments, sly digs and gusty jokes, they are always born of the moment and seldom repeated. There is no dreary attempt to raise a laugh with stale cleverness.

Their names alone are guarantee of their lineage, of pedigrees longer and blood more ancient than that of half the people who add strange decoration to our peerage. D'Wit and Mussett are the one Dutch and the other Huguenot, and their descendants to-day are fishermen-fowlers, oystermen and yacht skippers, village capitalists who own their own small ships, their own oyster "lays," and call no man master. Pewter and Cant, Hedgecock and Spitty, Heard and Levett, Sycamore and Turner—here are names that are pure Essex and coastal Essex, too. That great yacht skipper, Captain Sycamore of Brightlingsea, will write his name forever in the salty annals of the America's Cup Races, even as Captain Turner was skipper of *Britannia*, that lovely and royal craft which now lies sunk at rest on the floor of the Channel. And it was Captain Heard who mastered the Atlantic crossing in the dismasted *Endeavour*, a feat of superb seamanship at which all the world wondered and of which he merely said to me: "Ah! it was nothing. You know what these newspapers are!"

Was it not old Captain Spitty of Bradwell Waterside who sprang overboard in a January wind at the age of eighty odd and saved a drowning man, his fourth or fifth, I never knew which? As for that, my dear old friend, "Admiral" Bill Wyatt, that artist among shipwrights who is eighty, will tell you that he can still bicycle to London, walk ten miles, drink a gallon of ale, ride a donkey, build a boat, shoot a duck—and sail and win a race in his famous fifty-year-old smack *Unity*. These are men indeed.

The deeds of the younger ones of their names will shine forever in the tales of the sea whenever men of minesweeper and destroyer talk together of the bitter years we have shed behind us.

Do you wonder that I love this lonely, lovely coast of cold tides and wheeling birds and the men who walk with the heroes of old Greece?

In them runs the old, wild blood of the smugglers and

pirateers, the buccaneers and the men who were at St. Vincent and Aboukir Bay, at Sole Bay when the Suffolk cornfields shuddered to the thud of the Dutch guns, at the Kattegat and at Trafalgar.

Their language is old as the Dane, distant in its roots as the Norman, redolent of Dutchman and Huguenot. For is not your "beever," that pint of midday ale, merely the Norman-French "boire," and is not the man who "flees" a rabbit but skinning it in a Norse word? And if his fitten are frawned by a roke which comes in on the heels of the haar after the dag has cleared, why then you may be sure that his feet are frozen because of the cold fog which the sea mist brought in after the dew had cleared. And that is a fine jumble of them all—old English, Norse, Danish and Lord knows what beside!

It is a land of yeomen and fishermen, a blend of two most English and most independent strains. Inland and up to the very sea walls themselves the land is held largely by yeomen—Seabrooks, Marriages, Speakmans, Goodchilds, Eves, Buntings, Guivers, Goldings, Hutleys and a score more. Their names alone are like a roll of English drums among the archers at Agincourt. They were writ on the manor rolls as freeholders and socmen centuries ago. There are few big resident landowners, but many big and small owner farmers. Where large tracts of land are held in one ownership it is usually either by a squire living in a distant county whose tenants go on from father to son, or by disembodied entities such as the Dean and Chapter of St. Paul's and the Universities. The result is a race of proud and independent farmers and small owners, good Englishmen and good sportsmen, mainly Conservative to the backbone, and staunch upholders of Church and State.

They live, as I have said, in moated halls and ancient manors, houses which bear names that are part of the heraldic glory of an England that was noble and beautiful for all its wars and clash of arms. Those wars, in which fell Bourchiers and de la Poles, de la Hayes and Bohuns, were wars of gentlemen and men-at-arms, and not the cold modern beastliness of remote massacre of old and young, women and children, which is the fruit of our so-called science, our boasted "progress"—a progress which seldom builds a lovely church or a stately house, but covers the land with the gimcrack standardizations of the speculative builder and the County Council architect, those monstrosities in grey brick and greyer slate which are the antithesis of beauty, the negation of that loveliness in design which is the truest tutor of men's minds towards peaceful things.

Go back down the manor rolls of these old farms and dreaming houses which lie within their moats and you will find the footsteps of half the great families of mediæval and Elizabethan England—William de Warenne, Earl of Surrey; Waldegraves and Wentworths; de Veres and Rivers; Tyrells and D'Arcys; Botetourts and de Boys; D'Acres and Howards. There are Norman names and Saxon names, Old French and Danish still alive in these coastal parishes as farm names. Was not Wymarks at Bradwell-juxta-Mare, the farm of Wimarce, the Saxon who held lands under Sweyn? And the surnames of men whose humble callings are on farm and smack merely emphasize their ancient descent.

I was looking not long since through old manor rolls of the lands owned in twenty-seven Essex parishes during the fourteenth, fifteenth, and sixteenth centuries by the Lords Wentworth of Nettlestead, by Sir John Wentworth of Gosfield Hall and the Wentworths of Codham Hall, Wethersfield. Although the Wentworths have gone and Codham Hall is but a farm and all that is left of the glory of Nettlestead, which once was a mighty house with moats and outworks and a park, is a stone gateway pathetic in a stack yard, still the names of farm labourers and village freemen endure. Long after the knights and the barons are dust, long after the joustings and the hawking parties are but mere colours to an antiquarian pride in vanished greatness, the same village names persist at cricket match and flower show, at coursing meeting and point-to-point. Whose the longer pedigree and whose the more enduring fame?

That perhaps is typical of most of England, or rather of that England which hides behind the hedges and is older, far older and lovelier than the England of factory and cinema. But I like to think that perhaps on these East Anglian heaths and coasts we cling tighter to our ancient blood, albeit we may lose our acres, than they do in many other countries.

For one thing, this Essex coast was never an appanage of London. It may attract its butterfly yachtsmen in summer, its Cockney crowds to certain beaches, but its winds are too searching, its waters too cold, its skies too bleak in autumn and winter to hold that ephemeral breed for more than a month or so of early weather.

No, it is a land which Charles Kingsley might well have had in mind when he wrote " 'Tis the hard, grey weather breeds hard Englishmen."

That is why I love it, why it is a personal and dear land, a land to uplift the eyes by day and colour dreams by night.

My memories of this misty coast are long and coloured, bright jewels of unforgettable dawns and dusks. Lying up with a long gun in the mist-bright reeds after widgeon on the Long Fleet on Potton Island, five and twenty years ago. Going in a punt down Gunners Creek off the old chapel at Bradwell-juxta-Mare which Bishop Cedd of the Eastern Saxons built in A.D. 660, with Walter Linnett after the geese—ten thousand of them, shouting like a football crowd out on the misty loneliness of the Buxey Sand and on the death-trap muds of the Black Grounds. The sight of a pair of sea-eagles wheeling high as angels above Langenhoe Marsh on a blue, cold day in January when the short-eared owls were hunting the marsh like setters and a bull groaned and moaned on the sea wall. An otter in the fleet in Maydays Marsh within a yard of my gun barrels as I sat hidden in the reeds. A great white stork strutting like a ghost in the foggy dawn on the Blyth Sand in Thames-mouth as Charlie Stamp and I glided in the punt out of the mist. Trawling off Osea in the good smack *Joseph and Mary*, with beak-nosed garfish and ugly "rokers," sea trout and bass all in the nets at times, and then that never-to-be-forgotten stoop of a peregrine at a fleeing pigeon off Steeple Creek and the marsh harrier who crossed our bows as we thrashed home against the spumy tide off Northey where, said Alf Claydon suddenly, pointing with his clay pipe, "My owd dad took a nestful o' ravens' eggs out o' them ellums where he were a nipper." For ravens nested all up this coast as late as the sixties, and even into the eighties.

Early dawns on Old Hall marshes when the starlings rose out of the reedbeds in the old decoy pond with a roar like waves on a shingly beach and sixteen wild swans came in from sea with a whooping of mighty, windy wings which made Valkyrean music in the cold sky.

Sleeping one February night in a bean stack under the sea wall at Weatherwick when the rats rustled all night long and the widgeon went over like a river of wings. In the dawn a fox stole up the dykeside and sat, listening to the tiny song of the redwings in the thorn bushes, and the carrion crows beat the muds for the punt gunner's winged birds.

Crawling, heart in mouth, through the minefield at East Mersea for a shot from a mighty long-barrelled seven-bore muzzle-loader—and, mark you, shooting with those old guns is to walk with the giants of the buskined past—at the brent geese flapping like ravens above the creeping tide.

Riding on old Robert, that wise and gentle old hunter with the lion heart, along the high sea wall at Fingrinhoe with the full tide flooding at his very hooves, the terns dipping, the barges sailing, and all the far marshes shimmering in the haze of summer till we came to East Donyland, that ancient hall, asleep in its broad moat behind sentinel cedars.

And then the fowling nights—nights in the punt when the paddles dipped in icy water lit by winter stars, and widgeon mewed, teal whistled and the pintail rode lordly on the dark tide. Nights under the sea wall with the geese shouting on the sands and the sky alight and alive with the whistle of pinions, the skirl of wild voices.

Other nights in "Mrs. Hones," on Mersea Island, that peerless club of wild-fowlers and fishermen where the pint pots go round, the heron winks in his glass case, the brass gleams in the firelight, and eider duck and flying fish, little auk and white stoats tell in mute taxidermy their strange tales of northern seas and tropic voyagings. There were nights there, not so long ago and never to be forgotten, when the bombers thrumped overhead. The bombs swished down and burst with shuddering blasts and the very wooden walls themselves surged inward and sprang out again. And "Admiral" Wyatt grunted: "Give me another pint, Missus. Shutin' havn't opened yet, but them owd Jarmans don't fare to keep no close season!"

I think too of the lonely old houses I love—St. Osyth's Priory, gaunt with the flinty, grey majesty of Norman tower and gatehouse; D'Arcy Hall, with its mediæval panelling and high Solar, asleep in its shining moat where the wild ducks nest; St. Clere's Hall on its hill above the misty marsh, its high-timbered hall ghostly in shadow, the moat glimmering under dusky trees; Bourchiers, pink-walled and eaved, ancient as any, looking to the creeks and the lonely sea; Barn Hall standing on its upland crest just where the devil "hulled" its timbers and commanded its Norman builders to rear a house.

And humbler houses, remote and unrecorded in the antiquarian journals, bare, black, boarded farmhouses lying, treeless and stranded like great ships gone ashore, far out on the endless marshes, within the bitter smell of the sea—Smallgains and Bitchhunters, Twinklefoot and Twizlefoot and empty Canny Farm; Marks and Pakards and Weatherwick and, lovelier, gentler places, Reeves Hall and Barling Hall, and the old decoy house on Old Hall marshes where we ate and slept and cooked our food and hung up our strings of fowl while the bullocks gazed with great eyes and lowering horns in at the door.

Loveliest and noblest of them all is Layer Marney, aloof and alone in its terraced garden beneath the benison of its chanting rooks, gazing down across silent fields and far marshes to the farther sea—a house of enchantments. There is in all England no lovelier herringbone brickwork than is in that tall, many-windowed tower which was reared when Hampton Court was built and, I will swear, no more truly Essex home with its ancient trees and ancient church, its great refectory full of eagles and bitterns, wild geese and rare waders—all the birds of this coast of enchanted wings.

I think, too, of that other vast and empty mansion which overlooks my own war-time white and red house which for four centuries has sat looking from its bowed windows at the scarred oaks of Thorndon Park. Thirty years ago, when I first knew that long, sweet straggling marriage of two villages, Herongate and Ingrave, which cling as though for feudal protection close under the tall trees of the three-mile park belt, there were deer in that great park, the biggest private park in all Essex. Pheasants crowed in the coverts. Wild duck quacked under the moon on those twin lakes, the Old Hall Pond and the New Hall Pond and, on that farther one, across the wide park, Old Childerditch Pond, hidden under hanging woods in a little valley of sweet, lost cottages, a valley that might have been stolen from Devon and dumped down here in Essex.

There was a lord then in the great bare, brick Hall that stands like a Palladian Pentonville, gazing out across its lakes and stag-headed oaks and bracken valleys to its own dim, massed woods, and beyond, far beyond, in a most lordly vision, across thirty, or it may be forty, miles of rich Essex lands, golden with corn beneath a Constable sky, to the glittering salt tides and smoke smudges of the Thames Estuary, and beyond that still, to the blue hills and umber woods of Kent.

The fifteenth baron of his line could gaze out across that noble panorama of an England which had known his ancestors for six centuries and know that square mile on square mile was his. His farms were held by the sons and great-great-great-grandsons of yeomen who had farmed and fought under the name and banner of the Petres down the centuries. He could say, with a modest, patriarchal pride, that in village after village on all that great 27,000 acre domain his cottagers slept secure under roofs which were watertight and cost them but a few shillings a week and were safe for their lifetime and that of their children after them. They did not turn their tenants out lightly or for a whim on those old English estates which formed so much of the stout fabric of our country life.

But that fifteenth baron of a family who had been good Essex landowners for close on six hundred years died of wounds in the first war against Germany for freedom. And, since the price of death for freedom was a crushing burden of death duties, Thorndon Hall and its wide park and deep woodlands of oak and hazel and scrawny hornbeams in whose hairy branches surely witches must squat, was sold.

To-day the Hall stands grey and empty, a voiceless shell. The house and park which once gave steady employment to two hundred and forty men and women, to-day employs, perhaps, a dozen. There are no deer in the park. I have not seen six pheasants in two years nor a score of rabbits nor half a score of hares. The urban golfer plods his way where once the great red stags belled under October moons. Daws and jays, crows and foxes, stoats and rats, in their verminous scores infest the woods, where once six guns could shoot two hundred and fifty brace of pheasants in a day and the men and boys of two villages had a good day's fun and a full day's pay, with lunch and beer, at "brushing."

My mind goes back to those proud days of 1914 when thrones and empires stood and civilization had not yet committed itself in a mad, suicidal race toward a mechanized and atomic doom in the mis-called name of progress. To a boy on holiday in 1914 that park of bracken slopes and jackdaw-noisy oaks was an enchanted place. Across the green in front of the old Green Man, where the waggish Charlie Rudkin is village king and mayor alike, a path led to high, wooden steps. They straddled a tall, oaken deer fence, a fence so high that no red stag, they said, could leap it. Within was a belt of tall elms, full of rooks, and birches, silver and shaking in the wind, and brambles glistening with blackberries and, beyond, the sudden, wild sweep of the great park. Bracken slopes ran up to tall oaks whose branches and gnarled trunks looked ancient by day and haunted by night. Oaks whose scarred limbs and stag-headed crowns had, like enough, seen Tudor foresters draw a bow at the tall deer and Stuart falconers cast off their tiercels and lanners at duck and partridge. In deep little valleys, whose sunny slopes held all the September warmth of midday, the deer lay couched in the tall bracken, their antlers showing and ears twitching at flies. Fallow deer with dappled sides and tall red stags, magnificent of beam and spread, whose fathers, no longer ago than the sixties and seventies, had laid half the foundations of the present enormous stocks of red deer in New Zealand. For Thorndon hinds and stags were shipped to Nelson in 1851, and with Windsor stock and Invermark blood spread all over South Island from their first "enlargement" on the mountains of one of my wife's kinsmen, McLean of Morven, near Otago.

Their grandsons cantered proudly up the slopes of Thorndon or grazed in front of the Hall in those boyhood summer and autumn days of 1914, when their worst enemies were the keepers with rifles at the annual thinning-out, or men on horseback who rounded them up and drove them into great nets slung between the trees when a "catching up" was needed for stock to send elsewhere.

There was a deer-shed where the carcases were skinned and cut up on the crest of the slope below the very modern villa of the present agent, and there was, and still is, a Deer Cote, round and domed and thatched like an African rondavel, built of split pine trunks and full sixteen or twenty feet to its peak. It sits to-day amid tall nettles and thick briars and thicker fir trees on the edge of a high knoll overlooking the coots on Old Hall Lake, a pathetic survival of the days when deer came trooping, two or three hundred of them, through the snows to be fed on hay and roots when winter bound the soil and killed the grass.

The last of the deer went in 1918 or thereabouts. To-day no more lordly sight is seen than a stertorous golfer puffing off his week's sedentary fat between green and green on turf which once knew the delicate hooves of hinds and saw the antlered majesty of red royals. For those were indeed deer of the true old English sort and no mere, undersized park runts.

But there are still badgers to waddle and grunt amid the eerie dungeon ruins of the Old Hall in the Rookery, where tall elms and mighty chestnuts strike their roots in the forgotten floors of banquetting hall and solar, of courtyard and kitchen. Only the mute and narrow bricks remain here and there to tell of the vast, long-fronted hall, almost a castle, with its range on range of peaked roofs and mullioned windows and corner cupolas which stood on that lower spur of the park hills above the vanished church of West Horndon, on whose chancel floor and altar site corn now grows. That old Hall was built when Plantagenet kings were on the throne. It grew, century by century, until it covered three or four acres of ground not including its forecourt and outer yard and stables and the great dovecote, whose grassy mound remains. It was of all periods, Gothic, Elizabethan, and Stuart, a vast conglomeration of a house wherein the Petres lived as feudal overlords, vying only with the Tyrells of that other vanished castle, Herons, which lay within its moat in a shallow vale a bare half-mile at the back of my old house.

But then came the Georges and a Germanic taste for newness in all things English, a scorning of the old houses and old ways. So they pulled down the old hall which had nurtured three centuries of Petres and built, a mile or more away in the west of the park, that vast and Palladian house which now gazes, empty-windowed and smokeless, over the deerless park and the crow-ridden woods to the crawling sea and the mute hills of Kent.

As you go from Herongate to Old Hall Pond, which lies in a valley of oaks and willows, you travel a footpath winding through harebells which dance in the wind like asphodel on an Ionian isle, and you pass, on the right, a deep dell. It is floored with grass of so delicate and lucent a green that only the incomparable Algernon Newton could paint it. And, for that matter, few but that delicate artist, who has full seventy years of pure beauty in his brush, could paint truly the empty, aloof desertion of that pale, porticoed house, lording its lordless lands.

Under a wild and windy western sky at sunset, a sky of apple green and pale scarlet, with purple fading into faint, high blue, the house stands with a pale dignity. It is pathetic in the finality of its empty, windowless desertion, a house neither old enough nor warm enough for tradition or a ghost, not fine enough to command magnificence nor bold enough to be austere, yet, for all that, a house of state, an eighteenth century echo of dead greatness.

The dell is a different matter, a very witch-wood of the older Britain before the Roman came. Its green floor is aisled and roofed by the twisted boles and hairy branches of hornbeams of singular age and incredible scrawniness. Their branches claw wildly at the moon and seem to mock, with ancient satire, the sun. It is a place of green shadows and shafts of sunlight that glance like lost fairies on grey trunks and that green carpet of short, fine grass. An other-earthly place where the fox slinks and the wood-pigeon claps his wings. At night the long-eared owl hoots to the climbing moon and the badger rolls like a pig on his unhurried way. You will not often see a child play in that dell, and never a squirrel. An odd place, ghostly and unreal.

Old men in the village call it the Menagerie. They tell a tale of two hundred years or more ago when the new Hall was built and the "Golden Lord" was reigning, he who hung all the avenues from Brentwood to the Hall with cloth-of-gold to welcome the George who paid him a visit of guttural congratulation on his new and glaring palace. They tell of this hornbeam dell being fenced about with twenty-foot iron palings, behind which prowled lions and tigers and other strange manner of ferocious beasts. Like enough there were lions in those days when half the great houses of England had each their private zoo—and a very commendable fad, too—but scarcely lions and tigers together. They say, these old ones, that their village grandfathers and grandmothers lay fearful in their beds at nights, trembling at the roaring and gnashing of the wild beasts in this Algernon Newtonian dell. Perhaps that is why the rabbits do not play there to-day, and even the green woodpecker forbears to flaunt his red crest and laugh his defiant mirth. Sometimes, when I lie awake at nights and listen to the curlew flighting under the moon and the foxes yapping under the old oaks, I fancy that I hear, afar off, the ghostly roaring of those Georgian lions. They are one with the ghosts of better days.

So when I walk in this great, once-wild, park beneath those same "scrubby, old, stag-headed oaks of no great height" which Cobbett saw from his saddle a hundred years ago, and despised, I mourn the vanished greatness of the Petres who, if they never gave us a statesman to remember or an admiral to commemorate, at least gave this corner of Essex long generations of good landowners who let their farms at low rents and their cottages for peppercorns. They have withdrawn to that older and far lovelier hall of Ingatestone, a vision of Elizabethan beauty, whence they sprang, and Thorndon and its villages are the poorer.

Soon the greedy sluttish fingers of the city will reach out and soil it all.* The snug, friendly bar of the old Green Man will be shrill with strident Cockney voices and the yellow walls and red roofs of that inn of rustic charms, the Boar's Head, which has a carp pond full of ducks to mirror its face, roses about its windows and a courtly, old-world Master of Fox Hounds as its next door neighbour, will, like enough, be a popular pull-up.

So I will go north by east again to the cold coast between old Roman Colchester and the salt marshes of the sea, where winds blow too keenly for speculators to flourish.

I will stop and hitch Robert, as of yore, to the willow tree by the pond at that rose-red inn of Tudor homeliness, the Peldon Rose, the inn which stands at the head of the Roman causeway to Mersea Island, the inn where the smugglers hid their casks in the deep pond and under the long sloping eaves; the inn that Mahalah knew; the inn to which all fowlers and men of the marshes repair, where the talk is of guns and fowling, of nets and boats and men; the inn that is part of the very blood and bone of this older England—our coast of the enchanted wings.

* Since writing the above Thorndon Park has been recommended under the Greater London Plan for inclusion in the Green Belt.

The Chair-maker

By H. J. MASSINGHAM

H. E. GOODCHILD, of Naphill, is the last of the Chiltern independent chair-makers who owned their own workshops, trained their apprentices, and did their own felling or buying, sawing, chopping, shaving, steaming in their own boilers and turning on their own lathes all by hand. His cottage facing the Common is a kind of family heirloom, and his workshop adjoining and contemporary with it began its useful life as a seventeenth-century cowshed. His tank for steaming the backs of his chairs stands in his own orchard, and he has even designed and made many of his own tools. His father was in the same trade and used the same workshop, though he did not actually make chairs, but adzed out the elm-seats. The chairs he makes are Windsors, Wheelbacks, Ladder-backs and others modified from Chippendale, Hepplewhite, Sheraton, and other eighteenth-century designs, and he has made them from the variety of trees that grow in his neighbourhood, yew, beech, cherry-wood, walnut, pear, apple, elm, oak, and chestnut.

Lastly, he belongs, I am convinced, to that very distinctive race which not only first colonized the Chilterns 4,000 years ago, but were the first British people to introduce a tradition of highly skilled craftsmanship which in one direction, that of stone-walling in the Cotswolds, has never been equalled down to our century, when the art is all but obsolete. This race is the Mediterranean Neolithic, the builders of the long barrows. But this is not the place for me to recapitulate the inferences by which I arrived at this conclusion in respect not only of Goodchild himself, but nearly all the other craftsmen of the hills who, like him, are long-headed, small-boned, dark, agile, supple, animated, and rather short of stature. I set down these things in brief as a prefacing indication that Goodchild fulfils all the conditions that belong to the traditional status of the regional English craftsman. All but one; he has no son to follow after him.

I had not seen him for two years, and when I was last with him just before the war, I had made an exquisite discovery

G

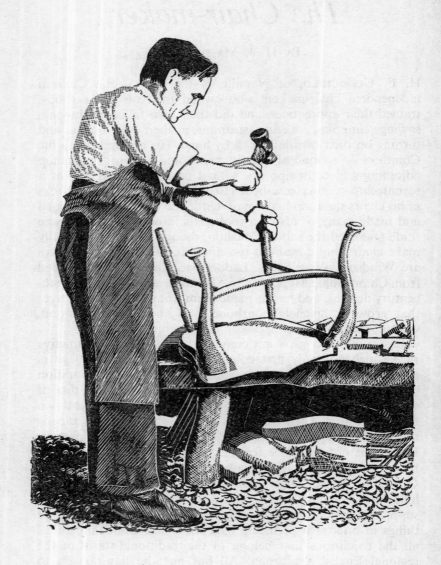

which had set the seal upon our growing friendship. More than a decade before I had first met him, I had bought at Heal's a pair of "Gothic-pattern" armchairs whose backs are similar to one type of decorated bar-tracery in fourteenth-century church windows. All unconsciously he had shown me a similar design in his workshop, and I learned that he had been the maker of chairs in one or other of which I had sat down to my meal for a round dozen of years. On the strength of this gracious bond between us, I had ordered from him a yew-wood armchair of the Chippendale Windsor type, and for two years I had heard nothing neither of him nor the chair. So I went over to see him, and from this point my chronicle begins.

Along the lanes on my way to him the hazels had shaken out a riot of flags. He received me as festively. He told me how worried he had been because he had not yet made me that armchair. But there had been an accident, he had been run down by a car; now, too, he was alone, his brother and his two apprentices had gone to the war, he could not get any more wood, and he was just filling in time with a few orders for plain Windsors from one of the more selective of the Wycombe firms. He was not making trumpery stuff (he would not know how to do that), but just ordinary wheelbacks, and so he had got out of the way of making the great chairs, the real chairs, the seats from which sages and elders and philosophers might deliver wisdom, at once meditative and oracular. He sat in one of them himself, what looked like a Hepplewhite Windsor with an urn back and cabriole legs, and made, he fancied, from a yew that had lived a thousand years. But he made just as good ones himself, sturdy enough to last a thousand years and with a touch of intricate pattern on the banister-splats. "It's child's play making these Windsors," he said as we drank a dish of tea together, "but in the old days I used to work on a chair till it was too dark to see, and then I'd bring the chair in with me, and when I had lit the lamp just sit and look at it." He loved it that it was his own, for its beauty and because his skill-hunger was satisfied by it.

After tea he took me to see some Carolean carving he had uncovered on the side of the open fireplace in the next room of the cottage, and in low relief on the cupboards for spices, the salt-box and what-not. I was amazed at the delicate and elaborate work, some of the finest and richest early seventeenth-century work I had ever seen, quite as good in its way as the carving on Jacobean oak bible-boxes or sideboards or middle seventeenth-century mule-chests, or even the church carving of Jacobean Croscombe and Rycote. Yet Goodchild's cottage had never been more than a cottage except for a brief period when it had been the village shop, while in the seventeenth century it was the only cottage on the village common, so that it could never have been other than the dwelling of a peasant or a very small yeoman. Goodchild had had to tear away a zareba of match-boarding and wallpaper to get at it, and so the whole dignity and honour of this poor man's palace had been restored to him, to him a prince among craftsmen, to him who belonged to a community not subject to the erosion of time.

Then we went off to his workshop. The same astounding litter of tools, benches, patterns and chairs in the making, piled to the very ceiling. Here and there a tunnel or runway threaded the wood-scree, embanked with chairs potential in every stage and process of purpose, bows, backs, seats, stretchers, spindles, legs, half-chairs, all but chairs, cliffs of them on either side. At the top-end, facing the front garden, ran long oak benches, not strewn, not even heaped, but smothered with tools and appurtenances of his trade of every shape and size, some traditional heirlooms, others made by himself—chisels, travishers, spoke-shaves, gouges, clearing-irons, double-irons, scrapers, mortizers, moulding planes, beetles, adze, tools enough to make seats for all the weary of the world. There were more of them hanging on the walls, though a space on one side was clear for a double row of splats in paper and wood, with their floral, scroll and curvilinear designs that he had modified from those that had pressed the backs of Goldsmith and Dr. Johnson. Indeed, Goldsmith's high-backed, top-railed, arm-curved Windsor which he left to his friend, Dr. Hawes, in 1774, was a much simpler affair than the chairs for which these splats were designed.

But there was a change, and I sensed it before my old friend blew the dust off the tools he was showing me, and before I saw the shavings lying among the tools on the bench, like wormcasts on a lawn. They should have been on the floor, in sacks, making paths, on the compost heap, anywhere but on the bench. A dust had crept over all that gallantry of creation, cinders had choked the furnace of the labour of love, weeds were growing over the grave of beauty's endeavour. The untidiness of an exacting ardour had been replaced by the disarray of an enforced neglect, and the workshop of a recreative tradition was sinking into the litter of Lethe. And with those brave tools on which a fine dust had settled like moss on the walls of a forsaken house, this man had made thirty thousand chairs. Thirty thousand chairs!

It was with a bitter naturalness that we began discussing what tools of his, tools he had made, tools he had inherited, tools he had picked up all in the day's work, I should have for my museum of bygones. He ran his fingers over them with that touch of intimate freedom that only the master craftsman possesses, and only he who has watched him at work can recognize. It was like an elegy to see him at it.

There was still something to do, yes, and still something to make, my yew armchair, and to this he reverted again and again. He had the very wood for it, he described the great cylinder of trunk with 150 rings in it, and the fine lines of his worn but sensitive and expressive face were creased with joyful anticipation as he foretold his malaise from the poisonous exhalations that yew-wood invariably gives out when it is worked. And he was for loading me with tools. But the adze whose haft was grooved with the pressure of his hands, and his father's, and his father's father's—I would not have this.

A great English craftsman never thinks of the past as we do, whether in terms of a disdainful progress or nostalgia. For him past and present are one, and time is a chain of recreations. I wanted a special banister-splat for my chair which he had adapted from a design of 1780, lyre-shaped with a centrepiece of Prince of Wales' feathers, but he wanted me to have another, even more intricate, which he refused to tell me about until he brought me the chair in person. There was no distinction in his mind between the old and the new; the works of the chair-makers were a single family in the fatherhood of time.

More than two months passed and then I received a letter from Goodchild telling me that he had booked a lucky ride and was bringing over the chair, the tools and sundries. The reason why I mention this letter is because all the "I's" in it were written "i," and this, like so much else in the nature of the rural craftsman, that stranger in our midst, is symbolic. It is the sign manual of a rock-bottom humility, a virtue as much a stranger in these days of man's mock-mastery as he himself is.

So he arrived and poured his hoard before me, including this chair of mine over which it had taken him two years to meditate and more than two months to make. It looks bigger than it actually is, though the back is three feet high and the saddle elm-seat roomy enough to take Dr. Johnson with plenty of space left over for body-movement to accompany the voice in the warmth of his dissertation. Dr. Johnson is the name—had he not a love for the powerful tavern-chair, which he called the throne of human felicity? All but the saddle-seat is of yew, that tough but brittle wood, so light in colour that it is called "white yew," waxed only and showing the knots and grainings of the wood like eddies and freshets in the stream. It is darker, a delicate interplay of light and shade, on the richly ornamental banister-splat and this, running the whole length of the back and very intricate in design, is a slightly modified Chippendale pattern of the great period of the master between 1740 and 1770. Indeed, it was in this period that the Windsor armchair with cabriole legs, splindles, stretchers and fiddle-splat of yew and seat of elm, first appeared in the history of English furniture and reached its perfect flower.

The splat-work is equal to the very finest in Chippendale's Windsors, and he may have taken some elements of the complex design from that of the Welsh love-spoons. The ogee-curved cabriole front legs are widely splayed where they join the seat and exquisitely notched where the tapering begins; these with the decorative splat are what bring elegance to the fundamental plainness ("plain" in the Miltonic sense) of the chair. The seat itself has soft undulations (like "the ribbed sea-sand") round its edges, fetched up by deep adzing, while the peculiarly silken quality of the yew-wood to the touch, glossed as though it were shotten, subtly adds to the flowing lines.

The breadth and spaciousness of this chair, its bold rich curves, its perfect proportions and balance, the gentle swell of the seat, the sweep of the arched stretcher that links the cabriole legs matching the forward thrust of the arms, themselves resting upon curved supports, the grace fused with substance of the whole, all go to make it as full a satisfaction to gaze on as it is a comfort to sit in. As I gazed at this work of superb English craftsmanship, I reflected that I now possessed a chair that expressed a miracle of continuity. The great chair-making tradition of the seventeenth and eighteenth centuries had passed through the Industrial Revolution, the Machine Age, the Era of Destruction, and across this triple catastrophe for the country arts, yet remained its own living self. For, as Goodchild put it, modifying the idea of divine right to that of impeccable taste, that chair was "good enough for Buckingham Palace."

After he had gone I sat down spellbound before it. For this yew chair is a perfect thing; it has achieved a synthesis and consummation of beauty and use. It has in it the quintessence of the country ethos, and in its origins the Windsor was a pure country chair. It is true that it had had a great urban vogue from the time when George III—Farmer George—saw one in a cottage and ordered with remarkable good taste a number of them to grace his palace of Windsor. They became all the rage in the coffee houses and tea gardens and pleasure gardens of Ranelagh, Vauxhall and Sadler's Wells; the gentry, the rakes and the lords and ladies of fashion sat on them at Bath and Tunbridge Wells. But up to this living day, of Goodchild of those Windsors it may be said—*finis coronat opus*—they have never in spite of all these town temptations been untrue to their country origin. My chair has a dignity and solidity that sets me thinking of the old tranquil countrymen I once knew who passed their lives in a seemly relation with their countryside, in an order and virtue lost to mankind. But there is nothing heavy about it; its curves have a freedom and generosity the reverse of stolidity. I can see in it the swift but leisurely processes of evocation, the judicious selection of the wood, the brooding over it, the instinctive sense of line inherited from generations of craftsmen, the eye-measurement and harvesting of ancestral knowledge working unerringly.

Yet there is that elegance about it, that delicacy rising out of its substance, that makes it something more than honest country goodness. It looks fit accommodation and equal welcome for a sage, a scholar, a tired peasant. The old solemn yew had lost nothing in becoming this chair. Man had responded to Nature; the beauty went on by transmutation. There is a restfulness about it that invites both meditation and recuperation. You could not imagine a man (and it is a man's chair) who sat in it uttering trivial, vulgar or malicious words. They would be words of understanding, yeoman words, well-chosen and deliberate, but with certain freedom of fancy and imaginative suggestion. Humour, too, but not wit. He would be a man of wise experience and maturity, one not prone to hasty judgment. And as he settled into it, the chair would impart something of the old, old life of the tree into him that had seen so much change and was itself changeless, stretching roots and branches a little wider decade by decade and absorbing into its dark shades the secret underground life of the great earth. For that chair is organic in every line.

And I, I had this prince of Windsors for nothing. Though I had coaxed, insisted, upbraided, not a penny would he take for it. I have known many craftsmen, and so am fairly well acquainted with their underlying though rarely articulate philosophy of values towards their work, and through that work towards the economic system which governs modern civilization. It is superfluous to add that those values and this system which is based not on the good thing made, but the good thing to be made out of it, are as incompatible with one another as chaos with order, the freedom of the person with the autocratic State. This attitude to price and to profit is not merely a legacy from the Middle Ages with their principle of the Just Price. It is man's natural relation with his work when it is based upon a sound tradition, when it is useful to his neighbours and offers him scope for the exercise of personal skill from which he derives his personal enjoyment in it, conditions all completely antipathetic both to modern practice and modern Utopian conceptions. Yet with this knowledge and experience I was so disconcerted by the point blank refusal of my chair-maker to accept even a just price for his masterpiece that I made but an ill advocate for my own argument with him. So I bided my time, and a few days after he had gone sent him a puny sum which I explained was for the cost of the wood and the special workmanship he had put into it. I waited, but there was no answer; I went on waiting, but still no answer, and so I determined to overcome the difficulties of visiting him and to see for myself how the land lay. For I would rather have had him pay me for possessing the chair than have risked his friendship.

He received me with great affability, and we sat down to his table and his greengage jam, and he told me how, when he was making my armchair, a famous designer had seen it and remarked that he had in vain tried to teach his workmen to make such chairs. A dealer had offered him a large sum, a very large sum, if he would make fifty of them. But, he had said, "I only make chairs like that for pleasure." Here I felt my face begin to burn. He looked at me with great earnestness, put his hand in his waistcoat pocket and produced my cheque. Then, with a gesture of self-effacing and yet royal courtesy, he handed it back to me, saying, "If I had taken this it would have taken away the memory of the pleasure I had in making you your chair." I said nothing. He went on to distinguish between ephemeral pleasure and the pleasure that lasts. He respected the pleasure of drinking a pint at the pub, but, as he said, it was not in the same kingdom as that of coming into the workshop of a Saturday afternoon and making that chair. Was I to deprive him of the pleasure that stays for the pleasure that goes? I thought of the planners who were busy in their London offices making plans for the countryman to have access to the cinema once or twice a week, conceiving in their machine-made world that a manufactured nepenthe must be the true solace for the infernal dullness of modern labour. For the words of Goodchild revealed another world as remote from the present as the moon.

So we talked, and it seemed that this man's feeling for his work and for the nature, quality and substance of what he worked in, was a truly religious one. But at the same time it was natural and creative. How illusory was the division we make between what we call art and what we call village craftmanship! Here was a man who was an artist literally to his finger-tips and yet was but a village workman. Subtlety was at one with simplicity. When I was leaving him he said something I shall not easily forget. He had enjoyed making my chair for one reason—because he knew it "would have a good home." The chair was as much a living thing to him as the tree it had come from. There was a difference in degree, but not in kind, between this and the refined animism of St. Francis, of Henry Vaughan the Silurist, and of Andrew Marcell's "My soul into the boughs doth glide."

I came indeed to look upon my chair-maker not only as a friend but as a part of my education. Through him I was picking up the pattern of a lost world; through him seeing my own world, the world of to-day, as having lost its way. Losing the meaning of work it has lost the meaning of life, which it must rediscover or perish as other civilizations have perished before it. It meant much to me, therefore, when I persuaded him to come over and spend another afternoon with me. It was late September, and we were walking round my garden, wondering at the variety of butterflies that were visiting the Michaelmas daisies. So very naturally we looked beyond the sport of the butterflies to the recreations of other days. You cannot talk to any authentic craftsman without going a journey of recollections. Recreation has become an obsolete word because it describes what people used to do, not what they do now. They do nothing now in their leisure; they have things done for them, mostly through machines. He told me that a man from London had once come to some meeting in the village and said he could not understand what people in a village did with themselves in their spare time. "Do!" said my friend with a shade of tartness in his voice. "We country people amuse ourselves, you townspeople pay to be amused." The decadence of the word "recreation" may indeed be traced back to its origins in the Puritan suppression of the old play-pattern by which work was organically associated with play. Ever since, they have drifted wider and wider apart, until the significance of leisure to-day is that it has nothing whatever to do with work.

My chair-maker is a lover of music, and so, he told me, had been his father and grandfather. But they did not listen to music in a concert room or by pressing a switch; they made their own music.

Recreation was thus another form of work because both demanded a measure of artistic skill, and Goodchild has often told me that he did not himself distinguish between work and pleasure. His work was his pleasure, his pleasure another kind of work. Once the villages about had been full of chair-makers; they worked five days in the week and went to High Wycombe on the Saturday to dispose of their work. He himself had had a horse of his own to carry his chairs or chair-parts, and, as the blacksmith was a mile and a half away, he learned how to shoe his own horse. This is the versatility of the craftsman who is never a specialized expert. These chair-makers used to grudge their Saturdays, even though they were paid for them, even though the jaunt was a change for them. They wanted to be at their lathes all the week. In our days, occupied with saving work, avoiding work, mechanizing work, scamping work, and hating work, these seem the doings of a people on another planet. Though they were intelligent men, nothing could have made them comprehend the modern concept of the Leisure State.

He told me, too, that the village boys after knocking off work used to congregate at the wheelwright's, the carpenter's, or the chair-maker's workshop and look on while the work was proceeding, no craftsman having any notion of a time-sheet. These instructional evening classes were combined with mild horse-play and bandied jests, as when the wheelwright would miss his blade when he was sitting on the draw-shave horse and dig the onlooker behind him in the ribs with his handle. Is it possible to imagine hilarity of this kind of vocational training in the inhumanly chilly classrooms of a State education? Then, one by one, the workshops closed and the farm-boy or the errand-boy or the butcher's boy or the juvenile apprentice, who had been educating himself by watching how things were made at a different trade than his own, became a lounger at the street corner, cracking inane jokes, gibing at the girls, and jerking out veiled slurs upon the passers-by. Play emptied of all content and reality. Goodchild told me he used to pass these progressive groups with averted eyes.

So we talked, rambling on from one thing to another, as is the way of village talk. But from it all emerged what I think is a great truth, that the right kind of work is play and the right kind of play is work. Since the connection between work and play has been lost, heavy trouble has come upon the world, and out of that trouble has loomed the hellish Utopia of the Leisure State.

It was six weeks before I saw Goodchild again, though he was constantly in the hinterland of my mind when I had his chair to look at and sit in. The art world is always babbling about self-expression in a work of art, which nowadays it so rarely produces. Well, I have the man in his chair since the qualities of that chair are those of its maker. When I drop my work and look at it, I can listen to "his pleasant voice, his nightingales awake" and draw into my inward ear faint undertones of that harmony of life and work his being represents.

There is an impression that the craftsman is a slow worker and that mechanical speed is an improvement on this defect of the hand-worker. This is due to a confusion between slowness and leisureliness; a craftsman is always leisurely, but that is because there is measure, economy and rhythm in all his movements and, knowing exactly what he wants to do and how to do it, he would make haste only to break the poise and order of his labour. Goodchild always appears to take it easy when he is at work, and yet had adzed 2,000 Windsor seats since last I had seen him, without help and without mechanical power.

I wondered then how he had escaped the maelstrom of financial furies and cut-throat competition of business practice to set up for himself. In a sense he enlightened me without my asking him. It had always been in his mind and purpose to find the way of becoming an independent master and, after his day's work he would try and figure out with pencil and paper on how little he could live. He calculated that, if a man could raise a small plot of corn in his bit of garden enough to give him a sack of corn (at that time, 11s.), that would suffice for his bread at the rate of two loaves a week. Vegetables from the same plot, wild-herb salads, keeping a few poultry and a pig, might see him through. Another thing he said gave me a further clue. He had gone to church one morning, and the text of the sermon was, "Where your heart is, there is your treasure also." Those words had been a kind of sign to him ever since. So by a frugality equivalent to semi-starvation, so by courage and unremitting toil, so by sheer passion for the good thing well done, he had disentangled himself from the dark jungle of modern business.

Yet how had he done it? For the more beautiful the chair he makes, the less he charges for it; he fixes his own price for it, and if he is offered double for it he would sooner not sell it at all. It is because he recognizes the true value of his work that he will charge so much and no more. And if he loves a man as by some mystery of the spirit he loves me, he will make a superlative chair and take nothing for it. How can a man like him, so utterly remote from the modern world, survive it? How can a man who takes nothing for something escape pauperdom in a world where chaos and system both are based on getting something for nothing? But nothing will budge him; the value of a thing is above money. What is the monetary value of the songs of Feste the Clown? By a yet more inexplicable motion of the spirit, the right value he has set upon himself and his work is what has won him his place as the master-man, his modest independence, his power of choice in what he will make and how he will make it. He can make chairs as the great masters of the seventeenth and eighteenth centuries made them and in the armed front of a civilization that thinks nothing of the worth of the work and all of the gain to be got from it. He has won his little throne in the esteem of those who know him, the sole survivor of the foundered kingdom of Chippendale, Sheraton and Hepplewhite.

On the last day of the year I seized upon one more providential chance to revisit him. This time he expected me, but he usually prefers me to burst on him without any preliminary arrangement, so that I can see the cottage as "it is lived in." But his wife's view is different, as all women's would be. I prefer his way, for, when the rooms are swept and garnished, I miss the full bouquet of that cottage's atmosphere—in one room the gate-leg table and the Windsor chairs from the eighteenth century to his own, and in the next room the rich carvings of the panelled cupboards beside the open fireplace, all so expressive of this timeless man who, when he talks or dons his apron, belongs to a creative race which belongs only incidentally to one age or another. Even the bread-oven is there, and if it is no longer used, that is not his fault, but because no corn locally grown can be locally sold, and there is no longer any local mill to grind it. Progress has insisted that we shall now pay for the flour double the price for which the corn is sold and for nothing of its nutritive value, without reckoning the costs of transport.

As soon as we had adjourned to the workshop, he pointed out a beautiful cherry-wood chair (as fine in its man-made way as his own cherry-tree by the way of nature) of the Gothic Windsor type, with a series of round arches in the top-rail, dexterous chamfering along the sides of the seat and elaborate "barley-sugar" turning to the legs. It had been made by a dead chair-maker for his friend, also a chair-maker, and so the man had put into his chair a number of touches and extra members which Goodchild dilated upon one by one, his hand caressing them, his eye kindled. Somebody had offered him a large sum for it, but he would not take it, not because of sentiment, but because what had been offered was too dear—and he showed me a minute crack in the seat. This inflexible, almost dogmatic honesty of his is a kind of armour that he dons to meet the odds against his own culture in which good workmanship is a religion and a man will sooner go hungry than sell his work or his possessions for more than they are worth.

The cherry-wood chair led us to resume our former conversation about the cut-price competition in the furniture trade. As he talked he was adzing out a chair-seat with the very adze he had once offered me, a century old and grooved where dead and busy hands had grasped it. The exquisite precision of his every stroke, leaving a succession of thin ridges and shallow furrows as though the blade were a share and the seat were a field, made me see by demonstration as well as by the total integrity of his character that it was impossible for this man to scamp a job. Yet he had lived in a world where scamping was the mode of existence. The competition was so fierce between the rival firms fighting for the market that he gave me one instance of a Windsor that was cut down from 22s. 6d. to 6s. 9d. If the chairs were not forced down to the very lowest price, no buyer would so much as look at them. How could workmanship live in such a world? A chair was flung together. He described how a porter at the station had tripped when he had just loaded a truck and put out his hand to steady himself against the back of one of the chairs. Instantly the whole consignment collapsed. How could men continue craftsmen in such conditions?

Once more I wondered how even he could have emerged a whole man from the little Armageddon of commercial competition, and still further than he had done already he enlightened me. He was once a cricketer, and in one match had been bowled for a duck twice in the two innings from lashing out at a cunning slow bowler. He noticed the smiles of the fielders as he went out and resolved never to be so caught again. He became a stone-waller, and described with gusto how he had gone through a match from first to last wicket without ever scoring more than two runs at a time, and making thirty runs in all. That doggedness was one quality that had brought him through an age of commercialism, true to himself and his craft.

But the principal asset had been quite simply the soul of the man. He had never been apprenticed, and in his young days he was picking up a precarious living making Windsors for the

Wycombe market when he came upon a Chippendale design, which he showed me. It had a richly ornamental banister-splat and top-rail with scroll endings, not unlike Oliver Goldsmith's chair. This design he had adapted for a Windsor chair of his own, and from that day forward he set himself to become a little Chippendale in his own person, and not so little neither. "When I saw," he said, "how the old people made chairs, I just knew I couldn't go on as I was doing"—and he spoke of the old chair-makers of the Chippendale school not with respect, but with a reverent passion, a glow in his face, an urgency in his voice and an animation derived deep down from that Neolithic race whence he may well be descended. That expressiveness of his lent a double weight to his words. My yew armchair had had something of the same effect upon him as his first Chippendale. Through it his spirit had undergone a second rebirth.

Goodchild may thus be considered a messenger from one world to another; he brings us news of that old race of English craftsmen, old as Stonehenge and young as yesterday, but doomed very soon to extinction. But the death of the craftsman will also mean the death of society, since man cannot live by bread alone. Do he so and he shall lack even bread.

Reproduced from "Men of Earth" (Collins).

American Uncles*

By Peter Howard

THIS is the quiet ploughland of old England, one of the most peaceful areas on earth, which was used to win the greatest war in human history. From the midst of these wheatlands and meadows, from among the centuries-old cottages, with their straw thatch and oak beams, the huge bomber fleets were airborne which pulped the heart of Hitler's Reich.

In these Eastern Counties the Pilgrim Fathers gathered and sailed away to build a new world. To these Eastern Counties their twentieth-century Pilgrim Sons returned to free the old world from tyranny.

Few of us in East Anglia have been to the United States. But the United States have been to us. We saw them come in our hour of desperate need—young men in tens of thousands, nonchalant, gay, confident and courageous.

---

* Peter Howard wrote "American Uncles" at the invitation of the United States Eighth Air Force as the last of their "Army Talks." It was circulated to the 250,000 men as they prepared to leave Britain for America and the Far East. It is reprinted here as a tribute to America and to the Eastern Counties of England, where this great Air Force found its British home.

Now they have gone home again, though many will stay behind for ever, a part of that free earth for which they gave their lives. And as an Englishman, one of a race which is said to be cold and proud, I would like to try and tell you very humbly something of what all of us who have been privileged to meet the men of the Eighth Air Force feel and shall feel for ever in our hearts about Americans.

The American story began for us long before the first Flying Fortresses or Liberators, the Lightnings, or the Thunderbolts swept through the English skies. It began one spring afternoon six years ago when clearly and steadily throughout two days and two nights we heard in East Anglia the sound of far-distant explosions. They were dumps being blown up by the remnants of the British Army before it was driven into the sea at Dunkirk.

We expected the Nazis to attempt an invasion within a few weeks. Men, women, and children, all of us, meant to fight. Yet we had nothing to fight with. In the area with which I was directly concerned, and on a likely line of advance if an invasion was attempted, we had seven rifles and 120 rounds of ammunition to defend a front eleven miles long and four miles deep.

Each night as my wife and I tucked the kids into bed, they would say, "Mummy, Daddy, are the Germans coming over now?" We would look at each other over their heads and make some joke as an answer.

Every evening after the day's work men and women met together all over the Eastern Counties and concocted home-made bombs, out of tar, gas and cotton-wool. We had to light the cotton-wool with a match and then throw the contrivance underneath an advancing tank in the hopes that it would catch fire.

We sweated away digging slit trenches and hiding places in the undergrowth beside all roads leading from the coast, so the Nazis would not see us before we hurled our home-made bombs at them.

We arranged meeting places in the woods if our countryside was overrun.

We hid food in places where the Germans could not find it.

We planned to set fire to our haystacks and burn everything of use to the enemy in the line of his advance.

All night long we kept watch on the church towers, at cross-roads, and at every important point in case the Nazis began to drop on us from the skies by parachute.

H

Then one evening all the able-bodied men were called to the village hall. On the floor were large wooden boxes. From them each one of us was handed a rifle and twenty rounds of ammunition. For the first time since Dunkirk we felt we had something to hit back with if they came. Our hearts sang a new song. It is a feeling I shall remember all my days.

These rifles were the first weapons to reach the Eastern Counties from the U.S.A. Lend-Lease may have been a subject of political controversy in the United States. Over here it was as if a friend had suddenly put a weapon in our hands at a time when our backs were to the wall and we had nothing but faith left to us.

*   *   *   *   *

All night long and every night the Nazi planes droned overhead on their way to London. For many months they were almost unopposed. We of the Eastern Counties slept on the ground floor and in the cupboard under the stairs, if we had one. Experience showed this was the safest place if the house was blitzed.

The German aircraft engines gave forth an eerie two-noted sound. If a glimmer of light showed from the ground they dropped bombs. Sometimes by mistake they bombed the reflection of the moon cast back to them from the lakes and waters of the fenlands.

The huge fires they started in London threw a rosy light on to the eastern horizon.

By day sneak enemy raiders roamed the skies and fled away again often unmolested. It was in those far-off days that the first preparations were made in the Eastern Counties for these vast airfields which presently were to launch the death strokes upon Hitler's Reich.

We in Britain built and equipped the base for the U.S. Eighth Air Force as part of our share of Lend-Lease in reverse. Many of them were placed on the finest farming land in Britain. Parts of the Eastern Counties of England grow heavier crops per acre than any other land in the world. And the surveyors sent by the Air Ministry to pick the sites of the bases chose land which was as level as possible. But the level land is often the best farming land, easiest to cultivate with horse and tractor, and the best farmers occupy it.

Farmers whose families had owned and farmed the same land for many generations found themselves suddenly dispossessed. They had to wait as long as three or four years for compensation from the Government, and when it came it was far below the market value of their holdings. But there was no complaint.

Bulldozers came smashing down the hedges and ditches.

Trees were hauled out root and all by huge steam engines, and if they snapped in the process their remains were blown up behind them.

Mountains of sand were carried and dumped in the middle of growing crops. Train loads of rubble from the blitzed areas of London were used to lay the foundations.

Tens of thousands of British workmen toiled through the wet and cold of winter weather, working long hours overtime, seven days a week, mixing the concrete, laying the runways and building huts and hangars.

Soon acres of concrete lay where the acres of corn had stretched before. As dusk fell, we used to drive around the deserted perimeter tracks in a car with sporting guns pointing out of the windows and shoot at the partridges as they came home to rest.

The first American arrivals, pioneers of the Eighth Air Force, technical advisers to help the British workmen in the final layout of buildings and tracks, stared at us in amazement as, looking like a load of gangsters, we rolled by in the gloaming.

*   *   *   *   *

Soon the first big bombers from the States, Liberators and Fortresses, began to arrive in the Eastern Counties. Then came the fighters. We who remembered the days when we called each other out of doors to look if we saw six friendly aircraft in the sky, watched them come sailing in by tens and fifties.

Village communities numbering only a few hundred people found themselves with several thousand Americans on their doorsteps, in their shops and pubs, and, very soon, in their homes. In many parts of the Eastern Counties the American population, since the arrival of the Eighth Air Force, outnumbered the British.

It was not easy at first. You found some of us cold and glum and angular, I guess, with our reserved ways and quiet, superior glances. And then there were the children—how they followed you in their scores and hundreds, clambering over your trucks and jeeps, like birds that follow the plough, with their eternal request for "Gum, chum!"

You must have found them a pest. But you never showed it. And the kids loved you one and all.

One day a jeep arrived at my farmhouse with four grinning urchins clinging on the back of it. One of them said with much pride, "Mr. Howard, 'my Yank uncle' has brought us all to see you." And a wee girl added, "Yes, we're coming every day in our jeep."

You were all uncles to the children of the Eastern Counties and, like most uncles, you were heroes, too.

*   *   *   *   *

So many problems of adjustment were met on both sides with a grain of humour and an ounce of tact. In our parts old Mr. Hollox had farmed his land for fifty years. In pre-war days, if one boy from the village walked over a corner of his field, old Hollox knew of it by nightfall. Now a huge perimeter track runs through the centre of his fields and a ditch which had been dug to carry most of the water off his fields was used by the base as a trash dump. Poor old Hollox used to go and look at this dump each day with a countenance so woebegone that his very beard seemed to whimper in the wind.

About this time he got in trouble with the local War Agricultural Committee for refusing to grow certain crops. This gave him another chip on his shoulder.

The commander of the air base wished to build a cinder track across one of old Hollox's beet fields so that the men could find their way home at night with dry feet from the village. He asked advice of a neighbour, who mischievously said: "Oh, go to old Hollox and tell him that you have never seen land so well farmed as the land around here—and that it reflects great credit on the fine work of the War Agricultural Committee."

The unwary commander did this. And old Hollox nearly dropped dead with rage.

That very night the commander got lost in the fields trying to find his way back to the base in the inky darkness. At last, around midnight, he came to a farmhouse door and knocked to ask the way. It opened with a jerk. There in the doorway stood old Hollox, wearing a nightshirt and nightcap, holding a lamp in one hand and a gun in the other.

When next day the commander of the airfield told this adventure to the neighbour who had given him the mischievous advice, the neighbour said, "I expect you found it hard to understand his broad Suffolk accent?" "Not at all," said the commander. "Mr. Hollox made his meaning plain enough."

Just the same, a few days later matters were arranged and old Hollox telephoned that they could build their cinder track.

*   *   *   *   *

So many pictures and memories crowd my mind as I think of those war years in the Eighth Air Force country.

Soon after the Americans began to arrive in the Eastern Counties a Piper Cub aircraft which was always having engine trouble became a well-known feature in the life of many villages. Day after day it would appear and land for temporary repairs—several times a day and always in the same fields. After about twenty minutes it would take off again, surrounded and cheered by swarms of admiring children.

The mystery was solved when it was discovered that the pilot always took the occasion of his breakdown to buy as many shell-eggs as the farmer on whose land he descended would sell him. It was an enterprising scheme to replenish the commissariat of one of the Eighth Air Force bases.

*   *   *   *   *

How to do the laundry for these thousands of men from across the seas suddenly planted in the midst of us? From the American angle I guess it must have seemed that all the villagers charged high prices and did not do the job too well at all.

But from the British point of view the problem was twofold— soapy and social. Our soap ration was barely adequate to keep our own hands clean when we came off the land at the end of our day's work. And socially, taking in washing was not considered "quite the thing" by the ladies of the Eastern Counties. It's a silly prejudice, but then human nature is funny stuff.

However, in village after village the word was passed around. "I'll do it if Mrs. King will," and "What's good enough for Mrs. Game is good enough for me"—so the talk ran.

Soon almost every village home in the Eastern Counties had a share in keeping the shirts, socks, and hankies of the Eighth

Air Force clean, mended and ironed. Maybe all of us didn't do the job just the way you'd have it done by mother back home, but we did our very best. And taking in the washing has produced quite a social revolution in the village life of the Eastern Counties.

* * * * *

Many of our villages are without a cinema, a club, or even a library. But every community planned and plotted some way to make our guests feel at home. In one village there is an old building dating back from the fifteenth century. The ground floor has bars on the windows. It was used by the old feudal lords as a prison.

The village ladies hired this place, painted it themselves, furnished it and decorated it. They turned it into a Welcome Club for the Eighth Air Force.

Every night volunteers served refreshments, and dances, debates, card-parties, and other entertainments were organized.

Few American airmen who spent their evenings at this Welcome Club making friends with the village people, could guess that they were being entertained in an old jail, which no doubt had been used to imprison many of those who were unlucky enough not to book a passage on the *Mayflower* and got left behind.

Clubs of this kind were opened and run by volunteers all over the Eastern Counties. Above all, thousands of homes were opened to the men of the Eighth.

What did the men of the Eighth Air Force think of the Eastern Counties? Not too badly, we hope. At any rate, many thousands of them married British girls in these years of endurance and victory.

* * * * *

Britain's Home Guard, over two million strong, at first armed with pikes and cudgels, finally with some of the best weapons of modern warfare, drilling in the evenings and at week-ends, unpaid for their minimum of 40 hours a month of training, stood ready for four years to fight the enemy if he landed on these shores.

The Home Guard was originally enlisted to defend their own towns and villages, each man to stand and fight and die if need be amid the streets and houses that he knew and loved.

When the big bases for the Eighth Air Force began to spring up like monster mushrooms all over the Eastern Counties, the question arose of who should defend them against possible enemy airborne attack. In most places the military High Command delegated this duty to the Home Guard, by then a highly skilled and heavily armed body of trained men.

Plans were made to muster in agreed positions and protect the bases at any hour of day or night that the "call-out" was given. So the village warriors of the Eastern Counties were prepared to leave their own homes and villages unguarded and to fight to the death in defence of the Eighth Air Force bases if the Nazi paratroopers had fallen upon us from the skies.

The Eastern Counties have a sense of eternal values about them. They are the great invasion belt of British history. Across these counties have swept Danes, Dutch, Normans, Romans, and many more, and have left their traces of habit and language behind them.

As the plough breaks the soil between the vast air bases, alive and throbbing with the amazing machinery of the modern age, it turns up ancient pottery, Roman coins, weapons of flint and iron, fossils, skulls, and bones.

When the Germans dropped their bombs around East Anglia it was often found that the old buildings stood the shock better than modern constructions of brick and stone.

Maybe the old buildings of the Eastern Counties have a bit of give in them. They swayed in the bomb blast and stuck together, while more modern buildings stayed rigid and disintegrated.

These old buildings have endured for centuries. Their bones are of oak, mostly old ships' timbers which sailed the seas in the days of John Cabot and Henry VII. The seamen used to exchange them with the farmers near the coast in return for victuals and supplies.

The flesh of the buildings, between the oak bones, is wattle and daub. Wattle is just bunches of hedge sticks bound together with withies. Daub was fashioned from clay, water and cows' dung to make it stick firm. It was mixed in holes in the ground, and these forefathers of ours used their bare feet for the mixing.

It was from homes like these, which still stand around the air-bases of the Eighth, that the men and women set forth to board the *Mayflower* just over 300 years ago.

In those far-off days almost all the farmers in the Eastern Counties used to hold a Horkey. This was a celebration in the barn each year when farmers, men and villagers sat down together to break bread, sing hymns and songs, dance and thank God for the harvest.

So after the Pilgrim Fathers made their landfall in the West, and in 1621 had gathered their first harvest safely in, with memories of the barns and villages of the Eastern Counties, now for ever left behind them, they held Horkey.

That was the start of Thanksgiving. And while in America the festival of family and earth has been maintained and enriched, in England we have let it die out.

This good old custom was revived in our neighbourhood in honour of the Eighth Air Force. Last harvest in our four-hundred-year-old tithe barn, beneath the Union Jack and Old Glory, over 150 guests sat down to celebrate together. The officer commanding the base was there and several of the pilots and ground staff. There was the farmer and his wife and children, farm workers and land-girls, the village blacksmith, the thatcher and the harvest hands.

Outside the giant bombers rolled on like thunder in formation towards the Reich. Inside, beneath the oak beams and rafters decorated with sheaves of wheat, golden-globed mangolds and hedge-blossoms, sat free men, united in a common crusade against evil and able to enjoy together the simple faith which turns to God when the harvest is home.

We ate home-cured ham, bred, fattened, killed and cured on the farm, salad, mashed potatoes and apple fool. We sat on together until the late evening, talking, singing the old songs common to both sides of the Atlantic, hearing recitations from the blacksmith and from others in the village.

And one American said, as he went back to base: "My, I've thought of home for over a year now, and this seems just like it to me."

*   *   *   *   *

At Christmas time many of the Eighth Air Force bases put on shows which the children of the Eastern Counties will never forget. Jeeps and trucks scoured the villages. The young guests were mustered and transported to the bases in hundreds. There was a huge tree, decorations, games, a present for each guest, any amount of candy which the men at the base had saved specially from their rations, and above all, large quantities of ice-cream.

When the jeeps and trucks came back to the villages in the darkness, the children tumbled out of them with their eyes shining like stars and their cheeks red as hollyberries with excitement. "Look what our American uncles gave me," yelled one little shrimp of six, holding out a huge piece of sticky chocolate to her mother. "Oh, Mummy, it was wonderful," said a boy of four.

Remember that many of these children, growing up in the war years, had never known a Christmas like that before. They will think of American uncles for the rest of their lives whenever the candlelight falls softly on the dark green branches of the Christmas tree and parties and presents are in the air.

*   *   *   *   *

On Christmas Eve parties of villagers go carolling through the hamlets of the Eastern Counties as their ancestors have done century upon century before them. Lanterns were not allowed in war-time because of the black-out regulations, but otherwise the traditional songs are the same. One Christmas Eve we gathered outside a sixteenth-century Woolhall to sing the old favourite:

> O little town of Bethlehem
> How still we see thee lie
> Above thy deep and dreamless sleep
> The silent stars go by.
> Yet in thy dark streets shineth
> The everlasting light;
> The hopes and fears of all the years
> Are met in thee tonight.

Presently, around us in the darkness, we heard the shuffle of feet and the whispers of voices. Without comment, men of the Eighth Air Force joined up with us. Soon there were fifteen or twenty Americans. Together we went the round of the village, singing a carol to the parson, the baker, the miller, the saddler, the wheelwright, the builder, and many other friends.

As we said "Good night" I caught a glimpse of one lad's face as he turned away in the moonlight. And there was a tear running down his cheek.

*   *   *   *   *

Well, the time came to say good-bye. The men of the Eighth

Air Force shared so many things with us in those last tremendous years which ended on VE-Day.

When a man has passed through the valley of the shadow of death with a friend at his side he never feels quite the same towards that friend as he did before and he cleaves to him for ever.

Our nation passed through the valley of the shadow of death and you came in your youth and strength and daring; in the majesty of your industrial might and power, you crossed 2,000 miles of ocean of your own free will to take that journey with us. How can we ever forget?

Every man in the Eighth Air Force has been an ambassador for his nation. And the job they have done in the building of new affection and understanding between our two democracies will live for ever in history.

You came to us in an hour when we were on the defensive with enemy planes in the sky above the Eastern Counties. You built up a strength so great that our minds could scarcely grasp the measure of planning and achievement as we saw those clouds of Mustangs and Thunderbolts, those multitudinous formations of Liberators and Fortresses lumbering into the sky morning after morning and returning near to dusk with their missions complete.

We passed from the stage of saying, as we heard the roar of engines in the early morning, "There they go"—to the place where we shouted, as the big birds began to drop in out of the eastern sky, "Here are our boys coming home"—because we have come to feel that way about you.

You may have noticed that not all of us in the Eastern Counties are perfect. But you have seldom said so. Perhaps that is why you make such good ambassadors.

Now, having won the European and Japanese wars together, we face the peace. Shall we win that, too?

Together we are bound to do it.

Plenty of people will try to separate us from each other in the years ahead, to stir up trouble between us, to get us spotlighting the faults in the other fellow while lightly skipping over our mistakes. But I do not think they will succeed.

A common language is not in itself enough to hold us together. It is just as easy, or even easier, to quarrel in one language as in two.

We have a heritage in common, also. But we have something more. As we of the Eastern Counties who were privileged to live alongside the Eighth Air Force for so long know full well, the ordinary men of our nations hold an idea in common. And an idea held in common will unite men of all nations, including our own.

Ours is the simple idea that men should be free to govern themselves—and that in order to be fit for this freedom they have to do, not what they are told, nor what they please, but as they should.

Some people call this idea "Democracy." It is, in fact, true democracy, though that noble name is wrongly applied in many directions these days.

Yet this faith in true democracy, held by the ordinary men and statesmen of our nations, makes us like-minded, however much we may differ in detail.

And in this age of division, disunity and hate, the future goes to the like-minded.

The Heron at Home and at Work

By Frances Pitt

THE lake was a long one. It
lay between green banks dotted
with tall trees, and in it were
two tree-clad islands. My island,
as I called it, the island of the
herons, lay at the southern end,
and not only were its trees tall,
but many were old and decrepit.
There were oak, ash and horse-
chestnut among others, but most
of them had seen better days;
yet they were vastly popular
with a variety of birds.

It was a keen March morning when I paid my first visit of
the year. The sky was blue, but a chilly wind whipped the water
of the lake into waves that broke against the sere yellow stems
of the previous year's bulrushes with sparkles of white foam;
yet rooks rose cawing from the trees and herons perched tall
and stately on the topmost branches, until they, too, took
wing and flapped off with measured beats of their great wings.

The bare boughs seemed full of nests, for there were a number
of rooks' nests in addition to those belonging to the herons.
Many of the latter were enormous structures that had taken
more than one season's work to accumulate, most of them being
of the historic mansion type, added to season after season until
they were huge.

But this was what one saw from afar, and I desired a nearer
inspection. Alas! there were thirty yards of water and mud
between me and the island, and no boat was available. The
water, it is true, was not very deep, but the mud was horribly
soft. There were tussocks of bulrush roots, and these were fairly
sound, but one was apt to slip off them and go down and down

into seemingly bottomless mud. I have seldom hated anything more than the passage of that thirty yards of water. I waded it bare-legged, I waded it in waders, and I waded heavily laden with cameras and other paraphernalia of a bird watcher and photographer, but I never liked it. I learnt every inch of the horrible mud, where it was softest and where it was not quite so soft.

I evolved a chart: you embarked by an alder stick, stepped to a submerged tussock, and felt cautiously with staff and toe for the next foothold. Thus half a pace at a time, testing the way with my staff, I proceeded with infinite caution, my eye fixed on the drooping branch of the horse-chestnut. When that was reached I should be going on so comparatively sound that one might almost call it terra firma. But oh! with what a gasp of relief did I scramble on to the really sound land of the island.

In the middle of the night I used to wake up and wonder if it was going to be a nice morning. Would it be suitable to go and try my luck with the herons, and should I manage the crossing all right? Then I shivered at the thought of making a false step and sousing my precious cameras; it was the fear of consequences to the cameras that gave me the worst nightmare.

But I will not harrow the feelings of the reader any further, and will say that the only mishap I had in the course of my many crossings—and I had to wade backwards and forwards several times at each visit—was when I slipped at the water's verge and sat down on the bank, gracefully depositing my impedimenta on dry land, but the spot where I sat was not dry, and I fear my language was neither parliamentary nor ladylike.

When I began my work with the herons the lake was low and the crossing without thrill, though it filled up later. That year I paid my first visit in April, when heron affairs were already in full swing, and a noise as of many typists at work on their machines in a busy city office came from the tree-tops. The young ones clattered their beaks in greeting to their parents and in demand for fish and yet more fish; the sound reminding me first of a Dutch heronry on the island of Texel, where the herons had their nests in a plantation of quite small recently planted pines; and, secondly, of the great cliffs of the island of Hoy in the Orkneys with herons nesting on the ledges, so that one gazed down from the cliff head, with the sea crawling hundreds of feet below, and looked into many a nest. The location of each nest was marked by a whitewashed area of rock. The young birds (it was early June) were standing like gaunt sentinels on the ledges, and their parents were flapping to and fro, but herons in Orkney and herons in Texel have not much to do with herons on the tree-tops of their island home in this English lake.

The next year I went early in March to the heronry, but the occupants were already busy, and as I stepped ashore many herons rose from the island trees and flew off with harsh cries.

I stared up at nests here and nests there. There were half a dozen great collections of sticks close together in one tall but ancient oak. There were over a score of herons' nests all told. The storms of winter had taken toll, and several family mansions lay on the ground, reduced to piles of rotten crumbling sticks. The trees were difficult from a photographer's point of view, but one nest was in good clear view from the ground. I put up a hide and left it for the birds to get used to, though, owing to the heronry being in a comparatively public situation, its inhabitants were not very nervous, and even while I was erecting the tent herons were flying around and joining with the rooks and jackdaws in uttering harsh and abusive sounds.

Now let us jump forward to an April morning, with trees budding into the tender greenery of spring, and thrushes and blackbirds singing. Tucked inside the tent, with cameras at the ready, and the horrid crossing temporarily forgotten, I stared through the peep-holes of my hide and studied the island, the lake and the bird life. What a busy spot it was. A chaffinch pair were courting at the back of the tent, the lovely pink cock flying after the coy little grey hen, to alight before her and show off his white shoulder patches. At the same time two coots were fighting in the water just off the island and making a perfectly outrageous disturbance. They fell over on their backs and clawed each other's breasts with their curious grey feet, while their ladies swam round as if cheering them on. Two wood-pigeons cooed, courted, drank and sunned themselves at the water's edge, and from overhead came the chatter of jackdaws and the cawing of the rooks.

Out shot two of the rooks. The heron belonging to my nest was coming home, and they gave her a too warm welcome, diving at the great bird and making her tumble and swerve about in the air in her efforts to elude them. The rooks were most spiteful towards the herons, and the herons despite their greatly superior size seemed afraid of them. They never attempted to defend themselves, but hurried back to their nests as hard as they could go. My heron came home in a rush, flopped on to the nest, and settled straight away to brood her eggs.

Pale blue eggshells lying beneath the trees told that most of the young herons had hatched, but the nest I had under observation was not so forward and the owner was yet sitting hard. I could not see much of her now that she had settled down, so turned my attention to other establishments. There were three large nests on my left, the nearest of which was even more behind time than my nest, for its owners were doing it up. They had, I think, got eggs, but the male, distinguishable by his extremely dark under breast and long head plumes, was very busy breaking off twigs, bringing them to the female and, while she put them in place, going off again for more. The guardians of the adjoining nest being away, he did not trouble to go far, but pulled pieces out of the walls and gave them to his mate with a lovely display of his head plumes and chest plumes.

Looking out from the back of my hide I saw nest-making material of another kind being gathered, for a tiny wren was collecting moss off a stone. When he—for it is the cock that builds the walls of the nest—had got a beakful he flew off to a nearby yew, whence he returned in a few moments and, regardless of my near presence—the back of the tent was open and he could see me clearly—went on with his work and collected yet another beakful.

The back view from my hide was quite as interesting as the front; not only did it include the wren and its activities, but I could watch the rooks and jackdaws. As we all know, jacks normally make use of holes in trees or buildings, but these two pairs had constructed bulky nests in thick ivy-clad trees. Unfortunately I could not get a photograph of their unusual site.

Several of the trees were supporting heavy growths of ivy, and out of one, from a point quite high up, flew a mallard duck, to alight on the lake and wash herself. On a subsequent day I again saw her descend, when she behaved in a very broody manner, and I have no doubt she had a clutch of eggs aloft, perhaps in the old nest of some other bird, or maybe in a hollow in the ivy-clad trunk. How would the ducklings fare? How would they get down? From what I have seen in other similar cases, I did not think they would get any help from their mother. In the case of a mallard duck that made her nest on the top of a very tall ivy-covered wall the old duck flew down and quacked below, and the family tumbled after her. Little ducklings are such light fluffy babies that they can fall without taking any harm.

To return to the herons, I had some grand views of the couple belonging to my nest. The male was a fine old fellow and a good father, too. It was amusing to watch him attending to his family, standing with his back to the breeze, when the wind blew his long head plumes up in the air and bent them forward over his bill. What a long beak it was, but he used it with great delicacy in his attentions to the young. By the way, it was the sight of two pale-blue eggshells lying among the bluebells under the tree that first told me the little herons had hatched.

While father was seeing to his children, mother stood, very tall and stately, perched on a branch beside the nest, surveying the lake with her keen yellow eyes. There was plenty to watch, from a herd of swans over a dozen strong ("herd," according to Dame Juliana Berners in her Boke of St. Albans, 1486, is the correct term for a company of swans), to coots, moorhens, and ducks. And there were occasions when military training operations made considerable disturbance on the lake, but the herons in general and my pair in particular stood the presence of a lot of men, plus much noise, with surprising equanimity. After much watching of the herons I came to the conclusion they were very easy-going, good-natured birds; for instance, neither the cock nor the hen belonging to my nest ever showed the slightest annoyance or resentment at the presence of a pair of tree-sparrows occupying a flat in a lower storey of their mansion.

I saw the pretty, chestnut-capped little birds fluttering about the heron's nest, and at first thought they were mere visitors seeking scraps, but soon I realized they were residents, having a nest in the interstices of the sticks that formed the foundation of the heron dwelling. It was amusing to watch the tree-sparrows going to and fro, and even perching beside their landlords, when they looked ridiculous midgets, but the herons never cast a glance at the mites—it was indeed dignity and impudence.

My couple afforded me some lovely memory pictures—tall, grey birds perched stately against the blue sky with white clouds racing behind them, and their whitewashed nest gleaming quite dazzlingly in the sunshine—but they were a sober couple and did not indulge in the dramatic greetings of the birds at adjoining nests. The pair next door were continually talking to each other with harsh cries accompanied by a wonderful showing off of their plumes. The female heron at another nest liked to bring her youngsters really worthwhile offerings, and regurgitated for their benefit a pike quite twelve inches in length.

What with one thing and another there was never a dull moment for the watcher in the hide. When heron affairs were quiet some visitor was sure to arrive. A great spotted woodpecker had a drumming-place in an old willow about ten yards away, and when it was not drumming I could see the flash of its black, white and scarlet plumage as it ran up and down the trunk of the tree.

Once the sinister grey form of a huge rat ran along the waterside and disappeared under the roots of the willow, and fishy shapes stirred in the dark waters.

The wood-pigeons, by now, had a nest in a hawthorn, and stock doves cooed in the horse-chestnut tree, though I do not think they had a nest on the island, for I saw them fly off to a tall, old and hollow tree in the park. Both jays and magpies came and went, accompanied by much abuse from the rooks and jackdaws, though the latter reserved their strongest language for the herons, which they delighted to torment. A heron flapping home heavily laden with fish was often the butt for a light-hearted frolic on the part of a pair or two pairs of rooks; yet, as I said earlier, the herons were long-suffering and put up with the attacks.

The young herons grew at a great pace. From every nest came the rattle of beaks, and the two visible in my nest were now well clad. They spent much of their time preening and dressing their plumage, using both beak and toe to comb their feathers. The heron, it may be remembered, has a serrated edge to its middle toe that is most useful for toilet purposes, enabling it to comb itself with ease.

I

But as the youngsters waxed, so did the time spent at the nest by their parents wane. To begin with, one or other of the old birds had been in constant attendance, but now the young herons were well fledged they came only to feed them and at long intervals.

The youngsters flapped their wings, danced on the verge of the nest, and again flapped as if in anticipation of the moment when their wings would bear them out over the lake and away to the reedy margin where the old birds waded through the shallows.

As I looked up into the surrounding tree-tops, where thick foliage now obscured the view, I could discern young herons perched on the topmost boughs, almost ready to depart but fearful to trust their wings. I tried to take a census, but it was difficult to do so with accuracy. As for nests, that was easier; I made it twenty-nine occupied ones the first year and twenty-one the following, with another dozen or more nests on the second island, which I could not reach. I was satisfied that the colony was in a healthy state and on the increase.

Reverting to young herons, the leaves on the trees grew thicker and thicker, and I peered through a veil of greenery at the final scene when my two, now "branchers," perched on a bough beyond the nest, flapped so hard that they found themselves airborne, and flew off in a wide circle. It was rather a crash landing that they finally made on the tree-tops. An aggressive rook dived at one. It uttered a harsh cry, took wing again, flapped across the lake, and the last I saw of it was when it was perched on a tree on the far side.

I pulled down my hide, rolled it up, packed up cameras and other impedimenta, and prepared to face the horrors of the crossing for the last time. I waded into the water, steering the now well-known course beneath the drooping branches of the horse-chestnut, towards the bulrush tussocks and the alder stick, but it seemed to me that far from familiarity breeding contempt, the mud was more bottomless and one sank into it deeper than ever before.

At last, after changing direction twice and thrice, I was finally across, to drop my belongings on the firm dry turf and look back at the island of delight. Rooks were flying like black imps about its tree-tops, herons were perched on the topmost spires and the great horse-chestnut made a wall of greenery on which its innumerable clusters of flowers looked like decorative candles on a Christmas tree. The whole was reflected in water that lay still except for the stirring of finny backs. In the distance stretched the lake, blue with the reflection of a blue sky, carrying the white swan herd on its surface—they were a party of last year's cygnets from the nearby Severn—and the whole was set amid banks of vividest green. It was truly a picture to live long in the memory.

It was an August morning, and I looked forth into the misty morning world at a dawn of still beauty. Grey vapours steamed from the turf of the meadow and from the glassy surface of the water of the nearly dried-up pond that lay on the farther side of the field. Ordinarily it is a nice deep pool where roach, perch, and tench have a happy home amid the tangled forest of water-weeds; but a long dry spell had had a dire effect, the pond was shrunk, until it now consisted of a mere puddle of shallow, dirty water surrounded by an expanse of sun-baked clay. The weeds had vanished, and not only were the luckless fish without shelter, but often their back fins were out of water while they were at the same time stirring up the mud. However, there was still a sufficient expanse of water to reflect the sunrise. The crimson and gold of coming day, slashed across with bars of purple cloud, rose to a dome of greeny-blue, and every detail was reflected in the rippleless mirror. The trees and bushes about the pond loomed blackly against the sunrise, making an ebony frame for its flaming glory, the grandeur of which increased every moment, yet its beauty did not hold my attention for more than the briefest of instants. A shape, a tall thin form, moved at the water's edge and was clearly outlined against the crimson water as a heron.

"A crane," murmured I to myself in the language of my native Shropshire, where the grey heron, *Ardea cinerea*, is usually known by the name that in bird books is reserved for *Grus grus*, the common crane. The latter formerly lived in our fen districts, but is now only seen in these islands as an occasional visitor at migration time. I am a complete ignoramus where etymological matters are concerned, but I have a feeling that our forefathers must have used the word "crane" for any tall long bird, and it certainly seemed very suitable for the grey shape that stalked along the pondside.

A freak of lighting now transformed the bird into a ghostly

white form against a background of reflected black trees, and
so it remained for a moment before it moved a step back,
spread its great wings, and rose with mighty flaps into the air.
Once more it became a dark silhouette, but now it was a shape
that departed with majestic beats of its wide wings towards the
east, where the dazzling radiance of the sun, rising as a crimson
ball above the horizon, blinded me as I tried to follow its course.

Such was my first glimpse of The Crane, but I did not give
him much thought, for I took it for granted that he was merely
a passing visitor. However, I was mistaken. When I looked out
the next day, on a morning as dull as the previous one had been
brilliant, it was to see him planing down from clouds of the
same grey hue as his feathers. He circled round on his great
wings, then with legs extended he dropped gently earthwards.
He alighted in the meadow and stood, tall, pale grey with
white front, and head erect, staring around. He gazed anxiously
about for some minutes before, satisfied at last that it was
safe to begin fishing, he turned and strode off towards the
pond. Carefully did he pick his way over its muddy verge and
then stepped delicately into the water.

My brother, who is a keen fisherman and takes much interest
in the inhabitants of the pond, saw the heron and cast a glance
towards the gun-cupboard.

"No! Oh, no!" I cried in answer to that glance. "He is worth
his weight in—in——" and I hesitated, when inspiration came
to me and I added, "his weight in port!"

Without waiting for a retort I hurried off to rummage out a
hiding-tent, for I had realized that if the shallow pond was
providing an opportunity for the visitor, it was also presenting
me with an unique chance of photographing an entirely free,
wild, uncontrolled heron plying his trade of Compleat Angler.

The tent was soon found and carried to the pond. The crane
flew off at my approach, but I had seen him take a fish, and I
felt sure he would return. I put the hide on the embankment
that forms one side of the pool and left it so that the fisherman
might get used to it. Next day I looked out of the window as
soon as there was sufficient light to see and immediately spotted
my friend. He was in the pool, wading just in front of the hide.
This was Sunday, September 26th, and, even if Sunday in these
times is no day of rest, it is at any rate the best day of the week
on which to take French leave of everybody and everything. I

gathered a cine-camera and a quarter-plate reflex and departed to try my luck.

With cameras in position I waited, staring through first one peep-hole and then another. There was plenty to be seen from the hide. There were a score of mallard, tame ducks that had their headquarters on the pond, and my pet geese, grey-lags, bean, pink-footed, and hybrid bean x pink-footed. They all came to wash and play—when they had finished the water was even more muddy than before. A party of long-tailed tits, danced about in a nearby bush, doing the most delightful acrobatics, such as hanging upside down by one foot from the extreme tips of the twigs. I was able to study the fairy mites in detail, noting their long tails, their grey, white and brown plumage, and in particular the broad grey-white stripe down the crown of the head. A portly blue wood-pigeon, with a very white collar, flew down and drank deeply on the opposite side of the pond. It plunged in its beak and took a "long pull and a strong pull," as is ever the practice of the dove tribe. Some jackdaws that also came for water took genteel sips, raising the head between each sip in order to let the water run down their throats. But I forgot pigeons and jackdaws when two great spotted woodpeckers on an oak tree across the pond indulged in a delightful game. They chased each other up and down the tree-trunk and then played hide-and-seek around it, when their black and white plumage, set off with touches of scarlet, rendered them very conspicuous. While romping they uttered a curious little chuckling call as if they were laughing at each other.

Woodpeckers, long-tailed tits, and pigeons were, however, forgotten when the heron arrived. He came so quietly that I did not see him fly over, but was suddenly aware that he was standing on the farther bank. He had evidently alighted out in the meadow and was now walking to the water. Herons seldom alight in the water if they can help it, having seemingly a horror of getting out of their depth. This is not because they are unable to swim, for I have seen one swim quite well, but because it is their custom. Heron usage ordains that the bird must descend on dry land and step cautiously into the shallows. Arrived at the pondside The Crane shook out his feathers and passed his long beak through them as if to tidy himself up before beginning business. I saw that he was a bird of the year and lacked the long head-plume of an aged bird, but he was a fine specimen and certainly a Compleat Angler.

Regardless of ducks and of geese The Crane stepped quietly forward, wading gently through the shallow muddy water, and picking up his feet so that he made hardly a ripple. He paused between each movement and scrutinized the pool with intent stare. He reminded me of a cat watching for a mouse. He was obviously expecting a fish at any moment. I pressed the button of the cine-camera; its mechanism made a purring sound, and I released the shutter of my reflex, which went off with what seemed a loud noise, but the fisherman paid no heed. I found that he worried little about noise, and was comparatively indifferent to movement of the front of the hide—for instance, I could swing the cameras in order to follow him about without alarming him—but any person moving within radius of his vision caused him to take flight immediately. The house was visible, and on one occasion a duster shaken from an upstairs window caused his hasty departure. He was not seen again that day. Fortunately he continued to disregard the hide, but on this first morning I could hardly believe my good luck. It did not seem credible that I was really watching a wild heron fishing at a range varying from twenty to ten yards.

The Crane stared steadfastly, then lowered his head a little, and with his neck extended to its full length made a point just as a terrier will point a rabbit sitting in a bush. Would the bird ever move? He did, with a sudden swift lunge that defeated the eye, and picked a small roach neatly from the pool.

According to many pictures and descriptions the heron transfixes a fish with the point of its rapier-like beak, but my bird used its bill like a pair of forceps, and very efficient forceps they were. Of course, a heron on the defensive and using its beak as a weapon against a foe would probably employ a different technique, when the beak would be a rapier in fact as well as appearance.

The swiftness with which the heron captured his fish was startling. It was like the pounce of a cat on a mouse, or of a hawk on a bird. But having secured it he again became deliberate in his movements. He held the silvery thing for several moments, while it flapped helpless in his vice-like grip, then by some sleight of hand, or rather sleight of beak, he turned it about so that he held it longways instead of across his beak.

It was now head downwards. He gave a gulp and another gulp and the fish was gone. He shook himself, looked a little thoughtful; but his hesitation was only for an instant, and in a brief while he was on the move again, stepping gently forward with extended neck on the look-out for roach number two.

In less time than it takes to tell the story the heron had a second fish, and it was as quickly disposed of. Like the first, it was a small roach between three and four inches in length.

The ducks, ever an inquisitive clan, now came swimming up, quacking, bowing and getting in the fisherman's way. The lanky visitor aroused their curiosity, and he found himself surrounded by a tiresome audience. It became more and more difficult for him to do anything, and at last he took wing and flew to land. Here he stayed for a time. He picked up and played with a twig. He preened himself and rested with his head sunk in his shoulders, as is the way of a well-satisfied heron. Unfortunately I could not stay indefinitely, so I raised the back of the hide, crawled down the embankment, and slipped away, leaving him still resting happily in the meadow.

The method of my departure gave me an idea. Each morning I put my cameras ready in the hide, but if there was no sign of the fisherman I returned to the house, where I continued with my jobs, keeping a sharp eye open for the bird. When I saw him I warned everyone not so much as to look out from the front of the house, and I slipped out at the back. I then made a considerable detour, approached the pond behind the shelter of the embankment, crawled up the bank and wriggled into the hide. For an elderly spinster of not-so-slim figure there are drawbacks to this sort of thing, particularly when strong thistles and remarkable thorny brambles add to the discomfort of the deer-stalker mode of progression. However, the feat was successfully managed, not once, but a good many times, and I had a series of interviews with the Compleat Angler.

The best photographs were obtained on a showery day when rainstorms alternated with bursts of sunshine. The Crane seemed extra keen. He stalked up and down the pond casting a vigilant eye first right, then left, and he paid no heed to the bothering ducks. Occasionally a heron becomes annoyed by too attentive onlookers, and I have known ducks receive nasty stabs, but this bird endured the quacking crowd with exemplary patience and displayed no bad temper. He continued his fishing and

came nearer and nearer to the hide, almost too close for the
four-inch lens I was using on the cine-camera and for the
seventeen-inch lens I had in place on the still camera, but when
he grabbed a fish I was able to get an excellent close-up of
him and his catch, the cine-film showing in detail how he dealt
with the fish.

This roach was a bigger fish than his previous captures, and
after swallowing it he waded off to the verge of the pond, where
he stood for a while with a decidedly after-luncheon look. He
tidied himself up, sipped water from a puddle, amused himself
picking up small things on the mud (possibly juvenile frogs
just leaving the water), and finally climbed the bank to find
a nice spot where he could preen himself carefully. He was
in the act of scratching his head when there was an agonized
squeal from beneath the bushes at the end of the pond. It was
a piteous cry, and was repeated two or three times. The Crane
stopped short in the midst of his beauty treatment, the ducks
turned and stared towards the bushes, and I, too, peered
through one of my peep-holes in an effort to see what mischief
was afoot. That agonized cry could come from but one creature,
a rabbit pursued by a stoat, and in another instant I saw both
hunted and hunter. The luckless rabbit was staggering down
the bank beneath the bushes towards the water's edge. The stoat
was just behind it, and leapt upon it as I stared. Again came the
dreadful scream and a scuffling on the mud. The heron on the
bank and the ducks in the water began to move. As folk in a
London street will rush to the scene of an accident, so did those
birds rush to see what was going on. The Crane raced with long
strides along the bank and the ducks swam at a great pace. If
there was excitement to be had they were not going to miss it.

By this time the stoat had undoubtedly killed the rabbit, but
I could not see exactly what was happening. In the light of
later investigation I think it must have dragged its victim down
a nearby rabbit hole, where it could deal with it unhampered
by an interested, inquisitive crowd. The ducks came back, the
heron returned, and all went on quietly about their affairs,
which in the heron's case consisted of more beauty treatment;
he scratched himself, using his long centre toe, which bears a
toothed comb, and no doubt distributed powder from his
powder-down tracts about his plumage, but I was too far off
to see the full details of his long toilet.

All that week The Crane fished the pond, coming early, middle-day and late, by which time the stock of roach was getting less, though there were still plenty of small perch. But perch from a heron's standpoint have their drawbacks, the chief of which is a strong, spiny dorsal fin, and he did not appreciate them. I saw him catch one, but drop it in disgust. The fish swam happily away. However, there were still roach, and good ones, too, in the garden pond, so the Compleat Angler turned his eyes that way.

By this time my hopes were rising high of achieving yet another photographic scoop, namely, a picture of two herons fishing side by side, for on hearing a sound as of a wagon-wheel in need of grease, I looked towards the pond and saw two blue-grey forms upon the turf. Was The Crane welcoming a brother? As a fact, his harsh cry must have been a warning-off notice, for the second heron hastily departed. I fear my friend did not extend a welcome to number two.

The Crane, I regret to add, showed a strong disposition to shirk his duties as a film star, choosing early morning and late evening for his visits. This, of course, was according to heron custom. Except in very quiet, unfrequented spots herons usually fish at dawn and dusk. Apropos of this, they must have amazingly keen eyes, for it cannot be easy to see a fish in muddy water when there is very little light. The late Dr. Francis Ward, with the aid of his remarkable under-water photographs, showed us how a fish may betray itself by the flash from its silvery side when it turns, and it is possible it is this flash that helps the grey fisherman of the twilight and even of the moonlight—I looked out one night, the moon sparkled on the glittering water of the garden pool, and there was The Crane striding across the lawn. He stepped into the water, where he showed as a black silhouette against the silver moonlit pond, and there he waited and watched.

For the next glimpse of The Crane, let us step forward some eight weeks to a morning when the trees and bushes, the grass and the rushes at the pondside, alike gleamed fairy white, for every blade and every twig had been bedecked with minute ice crystals. The grey mist that throughout the chilly night had hung in the valleys and on the lower ground was now dispersing before the sun, which shone from a pale blue sky upon the frosty scene. It shone, too, on the grey shape of "The Crane" as he planed down from over the tree-tops and dropped gently on the turf at the verge of the pond, where he stood and surveyed the scene, the world exquisite under a veil of hoar frost and the pond definitely frozen over.

The Crane, as I have already pointed out, was obviously a young bird, and no doubt this was his first experience of frost. The ice was outside his understanding, and he did not know what to make of it. He walked out on to it, slipped on the glassy surface, spreading his great wings to help him keep his balance, and then stared at the ice.

All this I watched from the house, from an upper window through which there was a good view of the pond, but now I felt was the time to get a nearer view of the heron's proceedings. Fortunately my cameras were already in position in the hiding-tent. All I had to do was to reach the tent unseen by the keen-eyed fisherman and crawl into it without disturbing him. I left the house by the back door, made a wide detour across the meadow, approached the pond under the shelter of its embankment, crawled up the bank and wormed my way into the hide. Cautiously I raised myself and squinted through a peephole, to see the heron standing just in front of the tent, but with his back to it, staring fixedly through the ice into the depths below. He was so near that I could study every little detail of his plumage even to the beautiful bloom on his well-kept features.

Very slowly the bird turned round until he was facing me, when I saw that he was tense with nervous strain, like a cat before a mouse-hole or a terrier pointing a rabbit in its burrow. He was watching fish swimming about beneath him. Suddenly he lunged, hitting the ice with his beak so that quite a loud tap was heard, and no doubt jarring himself most unpleasantly. He shook his head in a surprised and bewildered manner. He looked as if he was asking himself what had happened, how was it that he could walk on the water, and how was it that the water was hard and hurt his beak? With a puzzled expression The Crane stood thoughtfully for a moment; but soon movement in the water beneath him again caught and held his attention. Once more he stared entranced at fish passing below, with the result that he forgot his lesson and lunged at a tempting one. Poor fellow! It must have hurt, yet I had much ado not to laugh aloud, for his pained and astonished expression was so ludicrous. Moreover, it happened again and again. His beak must have been very sore. At last he stood staring through the ice, his attitude seeming to say, "So near and yet so far!" Then he shook his head, strode off to the end of the pond, and there took his stand, posed on one leg, his head sunk between his shoulders, as if pondering upon this incomprehensible universe.

A rime frost is usually followed by rain, and this one was no exception. The next morning dawned dull, foggy and mild. A gentle drizzle fell steadily. Photographically speaking, there was no light and photography was out of the question; however, from my look-out station at the upper window I noted that The Crane was on the pond. The pool still bore some ice, but there was water on it, and there was clear water at the verge of the pond. The heron was trying to walk across the ice, but its wetness made it doubly slippery. His progress was undignified. With extended legs held wide to balance him, he skidded and slid, but he arrived at a sedge-bed, where water rippled between the rush stems. For an hour or more he walked up and down on the edge of the ice peering into the sedge-bed, but what he got I could not see; however, he must have had some luck, because later he retired to the bank of the pond and there rested with a well-satisfied air. The fact that the drizzle had changed to steady rain did not seem to worry him.

It rained and rained, gutters ran with water like miniature rivers, and every ditch was a swollen waterway. The pond filled rapidly. It was no longer a muddy puddle, but a nice deep pool. The heron found this change nearly as embarrassing as the ice. Instead of being able to wade where he pleased, he had to be careful lest he got out of his depth. No heron will enter deep water if he can help it. Despite his ability to swim, he is nervous of making the attempt, which no doubt is the reason why he does not like alighting in water. It is, as I have already pointed out, heron custom to alight on land and walk into a pool. I will not say a heron *never* alights in the water. "Never" is a rash word to use; it is well known that every rule has its exception, but we also know that it is the exception that proves the rule, so I think my Crane was just proving the rule when he did drop down into the water, but this was into the shallow garden pond, the depth of which he knew precisely. As a fact, I saw him alight in this pool several times, but he was most careful not to take any chances with the deeper pond in the meadow. It was most amusing to watch him skirting round the comparatively shallow sides, but even so in water up to his under-feathers.

It was now that another type of trouble beset the bird, namely, competition. As already mentioned, a strange noise that reminded me of a farm-cart with wheels in need of grease, heard first in the stillness of the night and later in the early hours of the morning, had suggested to me that there was more than one heron about; indeed, I suspected there were four in the neighbourhood, but so far The Crane had had matters all his own way. It will be remembered that he chased off an earlier visitor. It was in the middle of Sunday lunch that some-one cried, "Oh, look!" and I ran to the window in time to see a heron duel in progress. The two great birds were dancing on the turf, their wide wings spread, and affording a fine spectacle.

I ran from the house, made the necessary detour across the meadow, crawled up the embankment and crept into the hide, but by the time I got there the herons had gone. All that was to be seen were two birds in flight, mere specks disappearing in the distance. The Crane was driving off number two.

After that both herons came separately; indeed, I recognized three visitors, but whenever two arrived together one chased the other off. They never fished simultaneously. Alas! their ranks were presently depleted. Visiting our local taxidermist, I found on his table a freshly killed heron. Where had it come from? I asked. It had been picked up, dead, from a shot wound, not three miles from my home, replied the taxidermist.

A few days later I had occasion to visit a mill on a pretty stream and was talking to the miller's son. "We shot a crane here this morning," said he. "It was after the fish. It was quite tame for a crane; we got it very easily."

I turned sadly away. Was it my friend who had been "got very easily"? My fears and surmises seem to be only too well founded, for no grey-blue visitor has been recently to the pond. However, I live in hope that it is only shortage of fish combined with deep water that is keeping him away, and that when the stock is replenished he will return to his old haunt; but in the famous words of a past Prime Minister, we must wait and see.

The Call of the Trees

By S. L. Bensusan

From my nursery window I looked upon the world for the first time with a genuine desire to know more about it. Beyond the garden stretched a long line of poplar trees; I could watch with infinite pleasure their quick response to the seasons. It was impossible, I thought, to doubt that they loved the spring and summer, regretted the autumn and dreaded the winter, just as I did.

The poplars, now long cut down to make room for villas, gave me my earliest glimpse of the beauty that lies beyond a well-planned garden; here flowers and shrubs were planted and taken away, drilled and ordered; there was no freedom to grow uncontrolled. Trim borders have never appealed.

I was still a small boy when I made my first acquaintance with a real wood, with centenarian oaks, imposing elms and stately beeches; it is not difficult to recall the strange feeling of affection and veneration, the secret resolve that if I grew to be a man I would have a tree of my own.

Fruit trees stood apart. They lived to yield an annual gift; they were in bondage to pruners and pickers; they did not stand on the same high level as a woodland tree; they passed their prime all too soon.

Fortune favoured. Owners of woods were kind; as the years passed some gave me permission to walk where I would and to justify my presence when gamekeeper or gardener came along. Down to this hour the woodland scene remains for me the most beautiful sight in the world, even a waterfall or a salmon river cannot challenge it. To-day, in old age I still look out upon trees, but the window is my study window, and the trees that mean so much to me are mine, in so far as nobody has any better claim to them. We learn to understand in time that the greatest landlord is no more than a tenant for life, often without power of appointment.

I began quite early to study the history of trees, thrilled to learn that the feelings they stirred in me go back to the dawn of time, or at least so far back that "the memory of man runneth not to the contrary." Aristotle told his followers that trees have perception, passion and reason; a Persian legend says that the first two human beings were created as a single tree.

Trees have had a big part to play in myth and religion, there have been sacred trees and there is a Buddhist belief that spirits take up residence among their branches.

So early as the book of Genesis we find reference to what must have been famous trees, "the oaks of Mamre and of Moreh"; and in the time of Abimelech there is reference to another oak, that of Meonenim; and another to "the oak of the pillar that was in Shechem." Some think that we should read terebinth for oak, but on the other hand one of the Mamre trees, says legend, was in existence in the time of Constantine the Great. The oak was sacred to Zeus and to Thor, the Druids sacrificed under oaks; at Dodona in Epirus an oak grove taught the nation. Clearly tree worship had had a part in mankind's search for God, and to many the tree was an epitome of human life. Legend says that St. Joseph planted a thorn that flourished for centuries at Glastonbury. I have a very old thorn in the heart of the wood, a corner so quiet that a vixen makes her earth nearby, and year after year in the recesses of that thorn the willow wren sings to his mate whose nest is probably somewhere beyond the tree and near the ground.

Primitive beliefs died in the course of the centuries, but the beauty and mystery of trees remained, and it became easier to enter into some sort of communion with them so soon as one has learned to believe that all life is one and that the only difference is in manifestation. The mineral has life, the experiments of Professor Chandra Bose show that it has something that might be described as emotions; the tree may well justify Aristotle; the insect world has its own cycles and ways of life of which we know little or nothing, but of all that is seen around us the tree appeals most, and with the tree I include the shrub.

Wordsworth wrote:

"And you must love it ere to you it will seem worthy of your love." This may be truly said of trees, for when you approach them with a feeling not far removed from affection, they will respond. In the darkest days of two great wars I have found complete tranquillity in my woodland, and among trees one is never alone. They have their own response to wind and rain and sun as well as to the season; one may interpret some of it at least. We may sense their trouble when a gale is blowing, their delight when warm days bring refreshing showers, their complaint when the burden of snow lies upon evergreen branches, their sigh of relief when the wind shifts their burden.

Most people are inclined to laugh at the idea that trees may possess emotions, but is there any lover of woodland who has failed to notice the fashion in which so many of its denizens await the coming of a thunderstorm. My poplars never fail to warn me, their leaves respond to slight preliminary gusts that do not sink to ground level, they shrink perceptibly, they quiver as though afraid. It may be that disturbances in the upper air account for leaf movements that, to some interested observers at least, express both fright and purpose. On the other hand their response to a warm light breeze in the late spring, when all their leaves are young, may well recall a line of the 96th Psalm: "All the trees of the wood shall sing for joy." Let us be careful lest we weigh the response of woodland to the pleasures and perils of its life in the balance of our own ignorance; it is such an easy thing to do.

There is a Mohammedan belief that when a tree casts its shadow it is in an act of worship: "At morning and in the evening the tree gives praise to Allah."

All over the older world trees have been held in veneration, and there was much superstition mixed with the reverence, indeed a council of the Church in the year 895 ordered the destruction of trees consecrated to demons. Kings and judges held trials beneath trees. The Christmas tree goes back to pagan times; to this day there are sacred trees on the Gold Coast—all these facts testify to lost beliefs of great interest and beauty.

This country has fallen from her high estate where trees are concerned. Julius Cæsar described it as "one horrible wood," but to-day we need all a Forestry Commission can do to hide the island's nakedness. Many years ago, in 1910 or 1911, I tried to interest the leaders of the Boy Scout Movement in a new development to be called Forestry Scouts, the idea being to reafforest England by the aid of the Scouts. The whole scheme was an elaborate one, and when General Julian Byng (afterwards Lord Byng of Vimy), to whom I first submitted it, was not interested, I approached *The Times* with the suggestion that they might make the appeal their own. Consideration was given to the matter, but the appeal was not strong enough, and seeing that no response was forthcoming I gave up the idea. Had interest been shown, our position to-day would have been altogether different where timber is concerned, for the oldest trees planted under the scheme would have had their thirty years growth. Perhaps I should have done well to persist in my attempts. Hardwood might be far off maturity, but there would have been all or most of the larch and pine we have needed so badly.

Because it is abundant in my modest woodland I have a great affection for the sycamore. This they say is not indigenous, though Chaucer knew it and Evelyn, that great authority, said it should be banished from all "curious gardens."

But I love the green flowers, so do the bees, and the wind carries the winged seeds so freely that I find saplings far and near. If not old in England, the sycamore is at least very old elsewhere, for the Egyptians of Bible times held it in high regard. There are no limes round me, so I miss the bee music there, but the sycamore makes atonement, calling to countless flying friends.

Down to a year ago I was the happy possessor of two or three fine hornbeams, but the best came to an untimely end during the war. It is pleasant to note how the parent branches hold on to their leaves through the winter months when all deciduous trees are bare, and it has the further advantage of being highly localised; very many English counties have never grown one. To-day only half a dozen small trees remain to me and they grow very slowly; for hornbeam at its best one must go to Epping Forest, where the soil is suitable.

The matter for wonder and reverence is that all trees, whatever their habit, contrive to carry on, getting their necessary first aid from so many quarters and in such varied ways. If a tree merely dropped its seed near the trunk, the end would come in a very little time, but all have helpers, the law that rules woodland sees to it. I have seen a jay and a rook drop an acorn in their flight and the red squirrel will do the same. I have a young oak sapling provided by a squirrel in this fashion a few yards from my summer house. Some trees are planted by birds which have swallowed the seed with the fruit round it, the ash and the sycamore cast their seed to the winds and the breezes carry them. Many trees are inhospitable to their own children, the seed that falls to the ground beneath them dies. This unfriendliness is part of a law we don't understand but may see in the working, not only among trees but among birds. Robins and kingfishers, to name but two, will not suffer their own children to live near them.

Down to a year ago fine old alders lined irregularly a stream that flows through my meadows. Then Searchlights settled at a corner of the field and the Air Ministry wanted signals in the wood, and in the destruction wrought officially and unofficially several fine alders went to their doom, quite unnecessarily. Their catkins and seed cases hanging to the branches through the winter months were a pleasant reminder of the spring, and countrymen speak well of the tree because they say its shade does nothing to injure herbage growing under it. Be that as it may, the alder is a gracious tree enough, and in years past a useful one, too, the charcoal it yields was used for gunpowder.

K

I had planned a path along the bank of the stream under the alders when labour should be available, but with the gaps now created, the walls must remain a plan. But in my mind's eye at least I saw something of charm and beauty.

The birch trees of which I have a sprinkling can boast a special fragrance, a delicate colour scheme and a very graceful shape, they have been called the ladies of the wood and belong to colder climates than ours; I am told that in the forests of Northern Europe they predominate. But my regard for this tree is due to quite another quality than endurance, scent or form—it is because the woodpeckers choose it for a home. On half a dozen you can see the circular holes in the trunk that reveal the woodpecker's work; if you find a fresh hole it is safe to look on the ground for the chiselled chips that testify to skilled workmanship. We have not only the green woodpecker, who laughs as he flies, just as though life were matter for laughter, but his cousin, the great spotted woodpecker, whose scarlet, white and black feathers strike such a vivid note and whose call suggests a miniature machine gun. Both birds are very suspicious, but by moving very gently and standing still at the right moment I have been able to watch each species at close range, and every year a green woodpecker brings her young, or a couple of them, to the lawn in front of the cottage, because there is an ant-hill there. Her nest will be in one of the poplars that is passing after a long life, the wood is light and soft, just what the bird is looking for. But she has been a careful mother—I cannot find the hole that leads to her nest.

Sweet chestnuts are at once a pleasure and a trial. They are a trial because they attract unwelcome visitors, all the local lifters of unconsidered trifles who raid the woodland to pick rhododendrons and bluebells in the spring, blackberries in the early autumn, and chestnuts a little later, in the intervals of setting snares. If they merely wanted a few nuts to eat there could be little objection, but I have found men filling sacks to take to town for sale.

I like to give the village school its chance on the floor of the wood, and then to see that floor handed over to the pheasants and the red squirrels. The nuts help very considerably to build the squirrel's winter store.

From my study in the cottage on the hillside I overlook the wood, and have been writing about trees visible across the valley. There will doubtless be some I have overlooked, but one more, the holly, must be included in these notes, for it adds so much to the scanty consolation of the season "when ways are dank and roads are mire." There are a score of mature holly trees scattered here and there, with many little ones between, perhaps destined to reach maturity, for they have few enemies. The holly maintains the continuity of woodland's colour scheme, and shares with gorse the privilege of resisting winter at her worst. Take the scarlet of holly and the gold of gorse away and we should be left with nothing more than the bright mosses that lurk in secret places; they bridge the space that separates the hour when the last of the deciduous trees sheds its lingering leaves and the hour when the honeysuckle calls to the still far distant spring.

The wood holds a few fine beech trees, and these are the more desirable because the beech is rare in this country of elms, oaks and chestnuts. They have many qualities, perhaps the first is the wonderful leaf mould to be gathered round the trunks. Carried to the light sandy soil of the garden, this is a great help to fruit, vegetables and flowers. I have often been asked to sell a few beech trees for the manufacture of chairs and other woodwork, but it is not good to sell what cannot be replaced; indeed, if it were not for the foxes, poultry might be brought in to eat the beech mast upon which the Saxons fattened their pigs. The beech is not perhaps a friendly tree, it suffers no neighbours and ground beneath it is bare, but it has family affections; note the fashion in which it protects the buds of next spring with the dried foliage of the present season. It is on this account that the young beech leaves are the most beautiful in all woodland.

During the war the Ministry of Supply demanded from me a larch grove with some 3,000 trees. They sent a dozen land-girls who, one hopes, spent a pleasant summer in the wood, and with two notable exceptions did nothing to injure their health by overwork. But the job did come to an end in undue course, and they left a scene of desolation behind them, as indeed they were bound to do.

Then a favourite bush, the elder, beloved of John Evelyn, took upon itself to step into the breach. To-day it has woven a bushy carpet over the waste, and as I write the creamy blossoms are everywhere.

There are many who despise the elder, still more who neglect it, but for me it has beauty as well as virtues. We make a delicious cordial with the berries, and keep it for two or three years in jars before use. But the claim of the elder on the lover of woodland is that it is first in the field with green leaves, appearing sometimes before the honeysuckle, and retains green leaves at a time when the most of our deciduous trees are bare. It is the only bush known to me whose leaves will keep flies away, and the old country folk will tell you of many medicinal virtues in flower, berry and bark, most of them forgotten. There are, or rather were, wise men and wise women in the marshlands who used products of the elder bush for a score of ailments. There were medicines, lotions, a special tea, wine and a cordial.

Many wise folk condemn both gorse and bracken, but I will do nothing to harm either. The bracken in the brightest season of the year is a joy to the eye for weeks on end, and a small clearing in it will enable you to see the most shy birds, to hear song on all sides, and to sense the atmosphere of woodland as nothing else can. Where the land can serve no agricultural purpose there is ample room for bracken, and where gorse is concerned who, having seen it in full flower when the rest of the woodland has surrendered to winter, would seek to destroy it? If labour were available I should be glad to prune and control the great branches, for they grow highly inflammable with age, but beyond this there is no need to do so; the colour note is not to be replaced north of the country of the mimosa.

The wild cherries and the mountain ash are among my favourites. In the spring the cherry blossom is so plentiful that the corners of the wood they favour look as though snow had just fallen. In the autumn the ground is covered with small hard fruit, and if one had the skill and the time it is safe to believe that the character of the yield could be changed by budding or grafting. The mountain ash provides a substitute for red currant jelly, when its pleasant white flowers have changed to lustrous coraline berries, but if it yielded no more than the spring and autumn picture it would be well worth having. There is much folk lore associated with the mountain ash, though not so much as there is with the common ash tree, if the adjective be permissible. Under the roots of an ash tree, according to mythology of Germany, hell was placed, the tops of the branches reached heaven, and in the shade of the tree the gods had their home, so that he who sits under an ash may be said to keep distinguished company. But perhaps the chief interest in any wood lies in the thought that the trees around have all been associated with strange beliefs that testify to their hold upon the mind of primitive man.

It is more interesting to think of woodland in terms of age-old beliefs than in terms of cords of timber; so much beautiful thought has gone out of the world, merely because business is business, that we do well to preserve what remains:

> "When science from Creation's face
> Enchantment's veil withdraws,
> What lovely visions yield their place
> To cold material laws."

To the lover of woodland every corner has its associations, and many a tree becomes noteworthy by reason of the part it plays in the great symphony of the seasons. Only for a few months in the heat and flame of summer does the wood reach completion. Then the leaves bear rule, the woodland choir already passing from song is hidden, young life may find cover from its enemies, even the keen eyes of the sparrow hawk and kestrel may fail to pierce the screen, but so swiftly do the seasons advance that almost before we are satisfied that the fulness of summer is on the land we may note the signs of autumn in the changing colour of bramble and bracken. The absence of some of the migrants, cuckoo, swift, nightjar, and nightingale create a great gap, all are leaving us for regions winter cannot invade, but so mindful of the place of their spring and summer sojourn that they will find their way back to it with another spring across a thousand miles or more. Without them the wood must lose a part at least of its charm. Does the wood feel this passing? Is it mere fancy or does the ripple of leaves when a light summer breeze is blowing tell of content as much as the sighing of bare storm-tossed branches speaks of suffering?

To those of us who spend all spare time in woodland, no matter what the season may be, there is some excuse for holding that it is vocal, that it expresses emotion, and that Aristotle was right. For those of us who hold that all life is one life, differing only in manifestation, there is an appeal in trees that evokes a constant response. We can't explain, for we can't understand the nature of the appeal, we merely feel and recognize it, finding enduring pleasure in a shadowy and undefinable association. We learn to know the trees when the various sections will be at their best and brightest, where to look for the brilliant mosses that are new year's first colour contribution to the woodland floor, and where the last of the wasps and hover flies will seek the ivy flowers after squirrel and hedgehog and dormouse have retired to winter quarters. A trifling knowledge enough but very satisfying. For we like to know where to look for the first sign of a new season, even though we are not anxious to see the earliest signs of the passing of the one we enjoy best.

There are those who love the winter woodland. One of our most distinguished landscape painters told me that trees reveal the full perfection of their form, naked and unashamed, when they have shed their last leaves, but I have never been of the company that can accept this. For me the late spring is best—best for colour, best for music. Nor am I ashamed to forecast the weather by noting the result of the spring race between the ash and the oak.

If it were possible, a woodman should be constantly employed to help the trees, there is so much first aid that they would welcome, but this work cannot be done and woodland must rely on birds and winds to maintain its life and receive no further first aid than is given when the ivy tries to strangle its unwilling host.

So soon as war started my woodland was in danger. The Ministry of Supply made a firm request, the Air Ministry a strong demand; there was no appeal from either. Then timber merchants wrote to say they were prepared to clear the ground and pay satisfactory prices, suggesting at the same time that it would be a very proper act to sell to firms that were really composed of patriots.

To one and all the 'tradesmen,' as we call them in Essex, went the same reply, courteous of course, but uncompromising. The trees must wait until one man's fleeting possession had been ended.

The Ministries were not alone in attacking the trees. The men of the Searchlight Station, or some of them, though told that the wood was out of bounds, declined to believe it, and went where they liked, merely assuring their army officer that they did nothing of the kind. They were greatly aided by the young women who were engaged in cutting the larches; they made some steps on the hillside to aid approach which was decidedly steep. Moreover, because the camp had only a restricted supply of coal, Searchlights helped themselves to wood so that I was painfully reminded of the first chapter of the Book of Joel.

Nor did trouble end here. In the middle of the wood in a part that a larch grove screened and elders may yet cover, there was a pleasant summer-house in which I passed leisure hours. It was not really attractive apart from its situation and equipment, for the roof was of corrugated iron, which is almost as offensive as it is useful, but at least it served a very pleasant purpose.

Came an afternoon when an airman ran out of petrol just as he was passing over the wood on his way to the aerodrome a mile away, the aerodrome that I have called Macbeth, because it murders sleep. He crashed; so did conifers and hornbeams and summer-house with its chair and table and cupboard. Mercifully the pilot escaped uninjured.

In theory the Air Ministry accepts responsibility and will pay for replacement, but no replacement is possible because material and workers are not to be found. The responsible authority says that it prefers this method to a cash payment, and who shall blame it? But I miss my summer haven and the sight of broken pines and hornbeams does not cease to hurt. . . . Very gratefully and humbly I admit my debt to woods, their gift has been the same whether in my own few acres or in the stately, well-tended woodlands of those kind friends who have given me their freedom in the years, now gone, when I could take advantage of it.

Stately mountains and great lakes, fast-flowing rivers that welcome the salmon from the sea can awe, impress, and thrill, but for peace, tranquillity and nearness to the heart of Nature, give me woodland, give me immemorial trees that watch the pageant of passing growth, that welcome migrant birds, that respond to the caress of spring and resist the onslaught of winter.

Thousands of years ago trees were worshipped or held in reverence, and who shall say that the poor ignorant man who could see his God in a tree was not better off than his descendant who finds the Deity in a bank balance?

Surely it is better to ascribe too much white magic to the woodland than to think of it in terms of mere utility as we do to-day.

Was Aristotle right when he said that trees have perception and reason, could one add that they have gratitude and a capacity for self-sacrifice? I would not suggest such a thing for a moment—but a night came in the autumn of 1944 when the flying bombs were crashing only a few miles away so that doors and windows rattled, and we decided that if the noises came nearer we would go to the Morrison shelter still unused. A few minutes later there came the sound of a Hymn of Hate that appeared to be chanted just above our heads; it was followed by a hideous crash, the breaking of glass, the fall of plaster, the collapse of doors, a mighty wind.

Nearly two hundred yards away one of the bombs falling to earth had struck the wood, and in that moment seventeen brave trees broke a great part of its force. They crashed and lay prone; all around them for a space of about fifty yards the leaves, branches, and undergrowth looked as though they had been through a giant's mincing machine. A part of the bomb carried on and came to rest a hundred yards down the wood.

Had the trees been sold so that there was nothing to resist the bomb, our home must have collapsed like a house of cards.

I remember how we went rather belatedly to our shelter and waited for a further message of destruction. One came, more than two miles away, but powerful enough to add to trouble; then the attack passed beyond our area not to return. My friends of a lifetime, oaks and elms, had saved us.

Hills of Enchantment

By HELEN HARDINGE

(The places and the people are all real but in disguise.)

THE house should have been for Hansel and Gretel. It was pale cream rough cast, with green window-frames and doors, and stood surrounded on three sides by fir and larch trees, opening on the south to moorland, loch, and a fine hill range, the foot of which was fringed with shining birch.

The place was enchanted, unique, solitary, and greatly beloved by us. Many wild, furious, wet storms broke over it and soaked mackintosh figures would be seen battling, practically on all fours, towards the house. Other days had the brilliant diamond sparkle of the Alps, the house stood on high ground. With bright sun, piercing light, air—fresh and rarified, all colours were translucent and pure. The children wandered out to the woods and hills on these days in their coloured jumpers, making vivid patches of scarlet, yellow, and orange, between the grey tree trunks of the woodland path. Gold-crests hung, like jewels, above the heads of those who lay beneath larch or fir. One enterprising bird got between the two sashes of a window and was extracted, unhurt, to return to its normal life.

To start with, we used to take servants with us, but they disliked the sounds of wild life—animal, not human—near the house at night, so we came with our children and friends only and the party grew and grew. We had a Scotch cook whose perfection, kindness, and good company made this plan possible.

We did a lot of bird watching and searching for flowers. This latter took us on some of the best expeditions. Later in the year the boys fished and the men went stalking. We learned to know the hills well, and in those great high, wide solitudes with their constant movement of light and colour and their changelessness of form, the words of the Psalmist automatically chanted themselves: "I will lift up mine eyes unto the hills." Or when lost, as was frequent, and finding unexpected heights rise before one: "Why skip ye so ye high hills" provided a variation. The Psalm, "The Lord is my Shepherd," was a faithful friend in the valley where the Highland river flowed and the oyster catchers and curlews piped. I know no country where the psalms dwell more in the mind or the words come so readily to the lips; especially, oddly enough, the metrical version. Perhaps that was not odd, but just due to the Sunday Service.

Rainbows played a great part in the expeditions: springing suddenly, apparently from a few feet away, in clear and vivid brightness; tempting the searcher after the fairy crock of gold, said to be buried where the rainbow touches the earth. The colours of the mountains seen through trees and beyond the shining loch, too, were the pure unearthly blue of celestial mountains.

There were many varied waterfalls: some romantic, overcast and overgrown, like Walter Scott's scenery; others bright and turbulent as the Highland rivers of Robert Louis Stevenson. But there was one which flowed from the melted snows and was the colour of pale green icebergs with a sheen of light cold blue. A pair of ring ouzel sang and chased each other there. The white foam and shiny green waters fell into the pool below a cataract and were still for a clear interlude before their next descent.

The writer remembers all sorts of days on the loch—solitary and silent in a light canoe when the pearl colours of sky, hill and water mingled in a glorious reflection like an iridescent misty bubble; a mirror for the jewelled halls of heaven.

Many loch fishing days were spent in company and with bigger craft. Once when, silent because of our task, two of us became hidden in one of the bewildering, enveloping mists of that country and all was muffled; suddenly, a strange, weird gabbling noise as of many witches flying on broomsticks and talking as they descended came to us on the water, and a gaggle of wild geese settled round us on their way North.

There were many bird adventures. The Goosander family, one of whom managed to drop down a chimney and get, all unbeknown, under a bed while the room was empty, where it caused consternation later by making flurrying noises at the human inhabitants. Great Northern Divers: Cormorants: Golden Eagles: and those fascinating flocks of Crossbills in their bright plumage, arriving from distant countries, with their strange antics such as walking upside down amongst the branches. Some friends and neighbours who were knowledge-able about birds and knew we were interested, used to tele-phone (they lived about eight miles away) and say: "The wild geese are flying North, they should be with you in about ten minutes," and we would leave our lunch and rush out, when we strained our hearing and later our sight, first for the strange, wild cry and later, watching the beautiful swift-moving forma-tion.

Snow, of course, was always dramatic. A dramatic sight, and also presenting an immediate problem, as we were easily cut off from supplies. In fact, all our dramas seem to have been caused by the seasons, the weather, or the wildness and capri-ciousness of the landscape. Sudden descents of mist on the mountain tops, distorting sight and sound, transforming the world immediately into an unknown, hag-ridden country, where we could hardly remember that once upon a time there had been sunshine. Drenched, cold, sightless; all sound an echo; the knowledge of the two hundred feet drop down the mountain crater became an immediate menace to those on the tops of the hills, and a cause of great anxiety to those of their relations (who had idly remained at the bottom) as long as the return of the party from the heights was delayed.

Once, the boys went to a distant loch to fish, travelling on difficult mountain paths; as they failed to return until after dark, we telephoned all over the neighbourhood so as to locate them in case they had descended by another road; then we prepared to light the beacon which should guide them home, and we got ready for an all-night vigil. They emerged, exhausted and bowed down by enormous pike. They and the pike smelt equally peculiar, but the latter proved delicious to eat, contrary to prognostications. They were cooked from a recipe of Isaac Walton's.

The most romantic moments brought about by social life were during the nocturnal drives home over the wild moorland by starlight, moonlight or headlights on the darker nights. The bright moonlight cast each shadow in sharp outline. The country was full of wild life. We would dress very smartly for the parties, in a great scramble, never having allowed enough time and all helping or hindering each other, plunging in and out of each other's rooms, piecing costumes together danger-ously with safety pins, lending and borrowing garments, brooches, etc., then bustling off to dine and dance. The dancing was extremely energetic and made one very hot. The mental effort was enormous if one's reels were acquired, as ours were, and not born. There was one Scotch family who had precision, elegance, timing and competence in all their dancing. They also had sufficient patience and kindness to cope with our enthu-siastic efforts. This high jumping gaiety was fun and the pipes had charm. But the road home was the best, watching for the forms of the deer, listening to every slight sound with the engine turned off while we stopped to look at the herds, quite close, standing immobile, then seeing them gracefully bound away. The great hills before us were sharply outlined: the dark wood through which we drove with its branches shadowed across the pale road; the gleaming river as we came out; the high, wide sky above; the bright shield of the loch and the amber radiance of a small lamp shining from the windows of that Hansel and Gretel house, the house we loved so much, and which, since the war, stands lonely, remote and in total darkness, unin-habited.

To guard the beam which shone for us, someone had had the

goodness to stay away from the party, so as not to leave the younger children, and to keep firelight and lamplight alive for our return. It was only the goodwill of all taking this task in turns, also the fact that there were so many parties to choose from, which kept our lamp so steadfast. Some enjoyed the quiet hours.

The drive home was the best of all: better than the pleasant fireside gossip on our return; the agreeable relaxation; the stacking of the finery, and decision to put the jewellery away in the morning, not to-night; settling into bed, knowing that the sun would shine soon through the larches beyond the eastern windows, making the cobwebs sparkle like delicate, quivering diamonds in the trees and on the grass, calling us to rise once more in comfortable old clothes again for a delicious breakfast.

Then the morning expedition to the garden to collect the vegetables. The vegetable garden had a palisade like an ancient fortress to protect it from the deer, and was a satisfactory secluded spot where it was easy to be overlooked when people were rushing about madly trying to find one.

Most actual human dramas unconnected with the weather turned on the personality of the nursery governesses who accompanied us. There was one fashionably inclined, a pretty foreign girl, who turned out to be a fiend to the children. She shook them with such energy that they lost all power to breathe and therefore to protest and then combed their hair with a violence which pulled out most of it. All this with the ambition, doomed to failure from the start, of making them look like smart little children in the "Bois." They always looked, and were, charming creatures of a shabby, tumbled wildness, untidy and careless with their very pretty clothes, and quite often extremely dirty too. None of their occupations led to polished cleanliness. And from the age when they rolled down the steep banks in woollen rompers to the later stage of corduroy trousers for both sexes and bright shirts or jerseys and occasionally bathing dresses, their lives remained definitely earthy.

So the smart foreign governess had to go and did so in the usual atmosphere of acute stress and nervous strain, the situation only being made tolerable by good manners and general insincerity. The children's aunt, to whom the negotiation of this change fell, was sincerely sorry for the departing one although disliking her particularly.

After that we had a darling, who was French and quite round, and who bore with us for many years. She used to bounce up and down the steep, craggy ways, and was wonderful at "first aid," which was often a great help.

We were all very happy. There were dogs, of course, but they had so much personality they must not be described or the anonymity of this place would instantly vanish.

The life, looking back to this northern home of long twilights and dawns and short, quiet nights, has a fresh feeling always dewy, sparkling and bright, and the photographs show a little of this. The latter ignore the easterly winds and the damp darkness of storms that frequently swept over us and led to many indoor enthusiasms. There was one hectic and agonised era, occupied entirely by the game "Monopoly," which was capable of lasting days on end, to the detriment of temper, character and the social welfare and amenities of all concerned. The writer never learnt this game but, watching the heated, flushed faces and listening to the incomprehensible but furiously angry arguments and noticing the impossibility of persuading anyone to come to meals, used to wish the weather would clear.

Then there was the caterpillar phase, which began outdoors and ended in the house. Many households must be familiar with this, but in our specialness the country we lived in was chosen by the Emperor Moth as his habitat. No less. This magnificent creature emerges, via a most distinguished cocoon, from a caterpillar only equalled in size, splendour and shade of colouring by the green Chinese dragons you see on porcelain. A Famille Rose caterpillar. This rampant creature could be easily found on the paths of the hills and brought home in triumph with what was supposed to be its favourite food, heather; then it was placed in a capacious jam jar and forgotten. These animals were remarkably rubber-like in consistency, and the writer distinctly remembers her sensations when, in the course of her, and its, rambles round the house she encountered one and placed her toe luckily, lightly, on it. She sprang back deftly at feeling the strange but totally unsquashed substance, and was pleased to behold the embryo Emperor quite unharmed! The writer was unable to take pleasure in housework for some time after that. It was almost as bad as the tadpole phase, but that took place in another house and does not belong to this story. One of the Emperors travelled to London as a cocoon in a jar, but, alas! the loss of his native Highland air made him unable ever to leave the cocoon, where he remained a woven mummy.

One of our successes was a place called the Moss House. It was in a green valley. Emerald moss, flecked sunlight, scattered scarlet mushrooms shown off by the brilliant-hued spongy ground, and tall trees all grew in the valley. The Moss House was constructed with much ingenuity where the ground fell steeply, so that its roof was level with the ground in one place and its floor six feet below was on the valley's level. Interwoven branches and moss made the walls and roof, and it was dry and snug inside; a small fire could be lit there. The Moss needed much care and renewing, and for specially festive occasions the outside was decorated with the scarlet mushrooms. Heather was used to bind the whole together, and so well was the Moss House concealed amongst the rose-grey tree trunks of the valley that we mislaid it ourselves sometimes—or perhaps it was just not always "at home."

The whole valley was changeable and unreal and made one think of Morgan le Fey and Merlin. The place was a joy for the children by day and a shelter to the deer at night. The haze of blue smoke from our bonfire was more intense there; the children's fresh faces and shiny hair were brighter; their red, apricot, rose-blue jerseys worn while playing games, a clearer hue. In and out among the woodland tracks, over the uneven ground, a figure would vanish to make an unexpected re-appearance; the purity of the bright alpine sun and air, the enchantment of the scene were unreal like a vision. Sharp, beautiful illusion: dear dream; every moment watching those darting forms and gay colours in the wood: the veil-like smoke, the luscious green of the ground—the writer would expect all to vanish, the scene to fade and disappear as in the enchanted wood in "Dear Brutus." But dusk only made all a little dim in a twilight of ghostliness.

Bonfires played a great part in our lives: to make, to sit by, to cook on, to gaze at, to keep the midges off us, and to put out. The putting out was a vital ceremony, as the peaty ground made it easy to start a running fire under the ground or a forest fire above it.

One of our expeditions was to a little grey cottage in open moorland. The mountains round were distant and a burn spread widely over the stones where there was a sandy beach. The jewel of this place hid in the grass a little away from our picnic ground which was chosen on the sandy beach. In this spot grew the lovely Grass of Parnassus, and each year we looked for and found the beautiful white glory of its flower. There were other similar joys—the high climb to the hill loch, where the witches lived on dark days and the heavens were reflected smiling on fine days, and which gave cloudberries as a reward and flights of ptarmigan to watch. The loch had a steep black perilous cliff on one side of it, creating darkness, echoes and the sense of a lost world. It was impossible to tell where sound was coming from. That was a terror of the sunless days and the mist.

One year, two of us went earlier than usual to this "story" house, and we had more time for excursions than later in the year and not so many duties to the neighbours. This was in May. We acquired a beloved pony which was named Ferdinand owing to his resemblance to a romantic bull of fiction. Ferdinand was a dear, and used to walk into the house. He was sociable and liked company. Two of us with Ferdinand chose a brilliant day to ascend the mountain of the lost loch, and after arduous climbings and stumblings by the way we came out on a small plateau of short, crisp turf where in glory stretched before us was that beauty of the heights—the Mountain Azalea. It is a brilliant colour and grows low on the ground, lying in lovely, dense drifts, like pale rose coloured snow. It was a triumph to find in bloom and a joy to see. After this invigorating sight we descended to the loch, which looked, that smiling day, like the surface of a bubble, blown by a child. On the way home we tried a short cut and got lost amid evil-shaped boulders and false echoes.

This year, owing to the earlier date of our arrival, the spring held another excitement. A fairly easy climb behind the house brought us to the Golden Eagle's nest with its one white fluffy eaglet. This was a curiosity, as the crags chosen by the bird are usually inaccessible. We behaved with the utmost tact. We endeavoured to make ourselves inaudible and invisible and, except on the first occasion, when we did not know the nest was there, we succeeded. The fledgeling was successfully reared —the first to live out of three broods which had been persecuted, maimed or destroyed, by traps or robbers. The crag was high and steep with a magnificent view, but one could get above the actual ledge where the fledgeling lived and gaze down at it, and one of us managed some photographs. Its growth and voracity were dramatic, and the debris round the nest nauseating to the senses. We dared not go often because of the famous long sight of the Golden Eagle. We did not wish to disturb the older birds who, though always invisible to us, might be watching our cautious movements, like the eye of God, from mysterious heights in the sky.

Our indoor and outdoor occupations were much interwoven. There seem to be very few human beings defined in this story, but that is because the immensity of the outdoor scene in which we lived filled our lives. There is another house where we later lived, and there the outdoor scene, though beautiful, was only the backcloth for the play of life inside the house. In this dwelling, which has a place in another story, the magic was indoors, elusive and personal and there was music. In the Hansel and Gretel house the only music heard was the Pipe of Pan, and that only once, early in the morning. The unmistakable reed pipe with its brief sweet song heralded in the loveliness of the morning.

One darling friend came often to visit us, and we used to have long rambling conversations over our domestic tasks, such as the shelling of peas or peeling potatoes which we did, sitting pleasantly in the sun before the front door. She is a saint, this lovable friend. We had vast sweeping subjects for our conversations. Faith and Belief were our favourites. We would produce our unbeliefs, which were many and varied. We discussed the confusing effects of "results" and whether one should judge by them. This sweet friend was entirely understanding, and maintained that "consequences" were no business of the individuals. The individual must do the right thing at that instant of time, the present, and the consequences, catastrophic or otherwise, were not the responsibility of that individual. All that was undertaken was a gift to God and must be done so that this offering was a possibility. If love, patience, sweetness, humour and great hardihood are the fruits of this belief, she had them all. It was not until much later that the writer learnt that fortitude, founded on the Christian faith, does enable humans to reach greatness. The accepted religion of Church

L

and State only occasionally rises to these heights, but great faith shines in some individuals, an unmistakable light to illumine the dullness.

People are afraid to talk of anything interesting. We were not afraid. We talked of everything—the stars above; God; why things made one laugh or cry; why the plants were green and the toadstools red; why when you mixed such and such paints they turned to other colours. We talked of telepathy of birds, beasts and fishes (lots about fishes) or rainbows; which statesmen had said and done this and that for England; how to bring up children and ride horses; treasure hunts and games; languages and their roots. And whenever we did not know the answer to why—why—why—we looked it up in the encyclopædia and became more disarranged than ever.

We had some tracking games, most of which ended in rows because, of course, no one ever found the tracks or trails left, and this led to definite friction between the track layers and the seekers. Besides lost tracks, a good deal of time was spent looking for lost dogs—the disguised or anonymous dogs. They were not supposed to lose themselves on account of the stalking interests, the house being situated in a deer forest. The wear and tear, anxiety and subterfuge these dogs gave rise to was enormous. Turn your head away to the telephone for a second to ring up the butcher—a gentleman who lived ten miles away and on whom one's existence depended—and where were the dogs—*gone*, carrying the rest of your day and half the night with them, also your peace of mind. No serious trouble occurred though, and now that we have all become so inured to real disaster, one knows no moment need ever have been wasted on anxieties so trivial. But there they are in the picture of this house—the disappearing dogs, and always disappearing at dusk, too, leading to alarums and excursions amongst the humans.

From bright dawn to green and lingering twilight the writer loved the beauty of the North. How pleasant to rest after long exertion; to lie in the warm grass, the air filled with the heavy fragrance from the blossoms of a solitary lime tree; the stream's song a constant sound; the wind stirring the tops of the fir trees, and enjoying the heather's honeyed smell; the oyster catcher's call from the river bed; the high white clouds overhead. The range of sense perception was glorious. Dried pine needles are very aromatic and so is bog myrtle. All blended to a dream as one sank into unconsciousness and a leaf of bog myrtle crushed between the fingers and smelt, as a pinch of snuff might once have been, conjures the whole magic back again; restores the scene vivid as an image in crystal. The clear countryside distilled this fine essence of itself.

As the year drew on and families returned to educational resorts, a different life began. The long lamplit evenings by the fire gave time for real study after the physical activities of the day had relaxed the body. At last one had time for reading of poetry and for looking out those half-baked botanical specimens and for studies which a practical and busy life makes impossible. All through there was an indoor wheel round which life turned, a wild hobby horse wheel—the spinning wheel. This was purchased in London, and no one of us had any lessons. The pleasant legend that the spinning wheel is soothing is nowadays a lie, whatever may have been true in ancient ages. Everything to do with the spinning was fun, except the wheel: collecting the wool, washing it until it became whiter than the fleece of Revelations, sparkling and dazzling on the grass where it was put to dry; carding and teazing was fun, too, although hard work; and dyeing in a grim iron cauldron produced astonishingly successful results.

All shared in this industry except when it came to the actual spinning, when one by one would steal silently away, terrified at the oaths and imprecations of the writer while she embroiled herself with the wheel. It was a remarkable object; it did everything except spin; it bicycled madly and played a tune and hit the spinner sharply and broke the wool (this ten thousand times), and made the most impressive cat's cradles, and caused the spinner's circulation to rise to bursting point so that she became dumb with rage. Only after major battles did it finally consent to spin enough wool to make one very remarkable garment. The garment, which took an immense time to fabricate, was beautifully, electrically warm: some said because of the passions that had gone to its making, and others because pure wool is always like that. Anyway, it was definitely warm and the colour of bracken at its most flaming. It was later discarded by a housemaid in London who did not understand its beauty, and its maker was stricken to the core.

Into this strange mixture of peace and confusion various outside elements came. There was a "great house" of the neighbourhood, not close, but within reasonable motoring distance. From here, one year, came a South of France contingent, accustomed to casinos and occasional gambols on the Adriatic shores. Their clothes held as much fascination for us as ours did amazement for them. They were kind to us aborigines and praised the Victorian elements in the furniture for their historic quality. They had a few of the hill paths flattened out because they could not walk on them, and then life wafted them away out of the country back into their worldliness.

The elements from the neighbourhood were not always like this. There were many visitors. The unexpected were sometimes a problem, as they were apt to arrive in the midst of occupations, natural to us but unnatural to them, such as the disentangling of fishing lines or a cooking party. The latter was the resource of a wet day. Into all this would be ushered, with insufficient warning, eminent and embarrassing company!

The least variable occupations were the vegetable garden and the household work, although the former was much affected by the elements. The sudden temperamental changes and vagaries of the heavens completely altered the order of our day. Always beautiful, it was never the same twice. Once, looking out fairly late in the evening, the writer thought, from the curious orange flare of light, that the house must be on fire. On going out, however, she found this hue came from low flame-coloured and smoking cloud, pouring from the west as though we were in the centre of Brunnhilda's field of fire. The wide moor was lit by this fantastic melodramatic light and reflected it.

The moonlight used to be so bright in the middle of August that long walks were possible, and we went on foot through the woods in a white brilliance with the shadows of branches laced across our paths. That was a good time for talking, too.

One or two of the party would not walk in the wood after dark because they were given to seeing ghosts and it had an eyrie quality—the footfalls silenced by the pine needles.

The writer had a different experience. Ever since childhood there had been a dream, a recurrent dream. It was simple. A long, undulating moorland road with a solitary figure: that was all. The first year the writer came to the house she found this dreamland road of childhood, and the dream ceased and has not yet returned. There was no fear attached to this recollection but some mystery, as the figure is still unknown although the road is now familiar and travels along it have given much delight. All real fears were, as they usually are, in actual experience, of a more concrete kind—for instance, adders were supposed to be our most dangerous enemy, and were fairly plentiful.

The hours of fright remembered by the writer were principally experienced on the enormous loch within view of the house. We used to take out boats on it for fishing or cross the loch for picnics and then light bonfires on the far shore. It could be idyllic. The boat was big and heavy, usually full of small children whose fish hooks got embedded in the most extraordinary parts of their persons and other people's, frequently incapacitating the oarsmen. Nobody actually ever lost an eye. This was great in fair weather, but in the twinkling of an eye, and much more rapidly than any transformation promised us by St. Paul, huge, apparently circular waves would rise up on a sudden wind. There were also waterspouts which went whisking cross the loch in spirals. The water was deep and icy cold and the shore always, at these moments, very far away. However, nothing worse occurred than aching arms from rowing against the storms, an occasional forced landing, and long swampy walks home with the prospect of rescuing the boat next day.

Sunday was a terrific day. We changed our clothes in order to descend to church. (The descent was only physical, and natural, as we happened to be half-way up a mountain.) Having changed the clothes, of course, the car would never start, and an oily interval took place, after which, much battered and dishevelled, we drove too fast to the service where we were supposed to arrive punctually. There was a fine preacher who took wonderful Old Testament texts and expounded them beautifully. The Scotch seem able to do this. There is an affinity between their hills and those of King David.

During the war the strong, lively and apposite poetry of the psalms sustained us in the great city of London, especially when the destruction was at its height. No journalist seems to have produced so apt a picture of the man who was Hitler as

the author of Psalm LV in the verses 21 and 22 of that song.
The eternal changelessness of human life and death made them
exceedingly topical. They revealed the everlasting truths and
were our inspiration, and it seems now in the peace problems
considerable prescience is shown by "Except the Lord build
the house: their labour is but lost that build it." Possibly,
"Their labour is but lost that 'plan' it" would be an appropriate
adaptation.

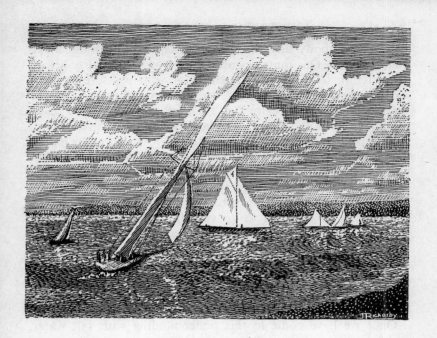

Saline Mixture

By LORD MOTTISTONE

AN eminent friend of mine, Sir St. Clair Thomson, has a theory
that man, like the other denizens of this earth, is of marine
origin. Our blood is a saline mixture, not dissimilar from sea-
water. This theory leads my friend to many important con-
clusions from the medical and biological point of view. I am
quite sure he is right, although I know nothing of medicine and
biology, because as an ignoramus in these matters I dare not
disagree with him on the grounds on which he bases his argument, but I am still more sure that his theory is correct, from
a lifelong observation of men and women who love the sea
and try to understand that strange and wonderful thing. Many
of my friends make their living that way. Others find in the
sea their chief joy in holiday and in sport.

　With all my heart I commend the sea as a place where the
best men and women can rejoice in life. Until it drowns you,
and this it only does now and again, the sea does everyone

good and nobody any harm, but of course you must make friends with it. One quite essential thing you must realize before you attempt to make your business or your pleasure in great waters: as soon as you are able to walk, you must get into the sea, and on the first calm day get some kind friend to teach you that this is the softest and best bed you can ever lie on. One constantly reads exhortations to the young of every nation that every boy and girl must be taught to swim. This is all wrong. Every boy and girl must be taught to float. Swimming can come later. It is supremely easy, once the fear of sinking has disappeared. One can practise all kinds of different strokes, some which enable you to go very fast for a short distance, others which give slower progress for hours on end, but the main thing is to learn the elementary fact that the human body is lighter than sea-water, and that if you will only treat your comrade the sea in sensible and kindly fashion, he will support you and bear you up, and the deeper you try to sink into him, the more surely he will sustain you.

Once we have come to this understanding with salt water, all life is different.

Of course this knowledge that the sea is your friend, and provides a good bed for you to lie on, except when it is very cold and rough, does not always have such dramatic consequences, but it does enable any one to partake to the full of almost the greatest joy in life—sailing. Nobody is too poor to enjoy the delight of sailing a boat, but nobody, whether rich or poor, ought to participate in this joy unless he or she can float and swim. Sailing one's own boat, however small, is indeed a supreme delight. It had been my happy fate to take part in, and enjoy to the full, sport of almost every kind. I have never been an expert, nor have I ever excelled, but the happiness and joy of riding a good horse, your friend and comrade in the hunt, of catching fish in salt water and in fresh after hours of hard work and disappointment, of rare moments of success at cricket and football—these are perpetual and worthy delights. But, as it seems to me, above and beyond all these joys is the successful completion of a cruise, however short, in a boat, however small, where by your own skill, patience, and courage you have made good, not in competition with others, but in using to the best advantage such skill as you may have acquired in enabling you to harness the forces of wind and tide to your purpose.

There is no other sport or pastime which is comparable to this. You are being made a better man all the time that you are engaged in it.

It is just for this reason, I am sure, that the sea-faring folk of Britain are the embodiment of all that is best in our character. I have lived amongst them all my life, and I can truly say that it is an ennobling calling. Whatever good qualities a man may have are brought out, developed, and made better by his contact with the sea. The mean things in him tend to disappear. I knew this all along from my contact with lifeboat men and fishing fleets, but proof, dramatic, complete, came when the first World War fell upon us. Strange, unknown reserves of courage and devotion were found amongst men and women in those desperate years, '14, '15, '16, '17, '18, but in no field of activity of our English life were these great reserves of strength found in so high a degree as amongst the seafaring men. You can hear the sons say to-day: "Father didn't wait to be fetched." Many returned to the Royal Navy, many to the Naval Reserve; all the rest, sooner or later, were off in trawlers or mine-sweepers, guarding the sea by which we live. There was a real problem in manning the two hundred and fifty lifeboats round our coast, for all the able-bodied men had gone. Old men and boys took their places. More than five thousand lives of sailors of every race, including our enemies, shipwrecked on our coast, were saved by these lifeboat crews. One particular case I remember of a rescue in a great storm, when coxswain and two other men were over seventy-three years of age and the rest were young lads.

Perhaps Sir St. Clair Thomson is right that man is a marine animal, whose blood is the same mixture as the salt sea which washes our coast, and is at his best when he is on or in or very near the sea. Of course, it is not given to every one, or even to more than a few, to have their home near the sea, but I would submit to my fellow-countrymen, and especially to the boys of England, that whenever they have the chance, they should get to the sea. There they can refresh their souls, and, while rejoicing in the good west wind, understand that it is by the sea that England lives.

And the people with whom they will spend these happy days are so good and genuine: boat-builders, sail-makers, fishermen, many of them lifeboat-men. They are the salt of the earth, these fishermen and seamen in out-of-the-way places round our coast. No danger daunts them. Nothing disturbs their good humour. A curious thing is that their readiness to help and their expectation of reward varies inversely, as the mathematicians say, with the violence of the weather.

I remember many years ago, when I was staying in Nottinghamshire, receiving a telegram saying that my father was very dangerously ill at our home in the Isle of Wight, and that I should come at once. A strong westerly gale was blowing when I got a train at Nottingham. Indeed our train was late, due, so the guard told me—no doubt quite truly—to the strong lateral pressure on the train caused by this great wind. So I missed the only train from London which would connect with the ordinary steamer. I telegraphed from Waterloo to the station-master at Lymington, asking him to arrange for a boat to sail me across to Yarmouth. When I arrived at Lymington town at half past seven on this winter's night, I found a wonderful old man, by name Doe, standing on the platform. I think he was about sixty-five years of age at the time, with white hair and very kind blue eyes.

He said to me: "It's blowing very hard, Master Jack, but I 'lows the wind has veered to due west or even north a bit. The tide has just started to ebb in the middle, so we shall fetch Yarmouth all right."

The thoughtful station-master had provided a loaf of bread, a large pat of butter, a flask of whisky, and a bottle of soda-water, in case, as he said, "You might miss the channel and get stuck somewhere in the river." So we boarded the boat, Doe and I, with my luggage, consisting of a bag, and, fortunately, as it turned out, an old-fashioned round hat-box containing a top-hat.

The wind was howling loudly in the roof of the station, but when we got on board in the pitch darkness in the little pool near the railway, we were under the lee of the houses, and had no difficulty in hoisting the mainsail. Doe had taken three reefs down in the mainsail, so little sail being left that I wondered if we should make to windward round the bends. I said so. He replied: "You wait till we get half-way down the river, Master Jack, and you won't think we've got too little sail." Then I took the helm, Doe cast off the mooring, hoisted a tiny pocket handkerchief of a jib, and away we sailed in the darkness down the river. Sure enough, when we had gone a quarter of a mile or so, we met a blast of wind of extraordinary power. It was raining from thick clouds, but there was a moon behind them, which enabled us to see the booms marking the channel.

She was an eighteen-foot boat decked forward, but quite open for the rest of her length. In the calm water of the little estuary we rushed along at an amazing speed. As Doe had foreseen, the wind had gone round just to the north of west, and so was just abaft the beam—that point of sailing which makes any boat, big or little, go its fastest. As we approached Jack in the Basket, the last mark going out of the river, I said to my friend Doe: "We shall have a bit of a dusting going across. Why not have some whisky and soda and a bite of bread before we get into it? You will find it all stowed in my hat-box." Doe said, "I doubt we shall have time," but he opened the hat-box. But for this fortunate happening, I should not now be writing this account of our adventure together. Just as he had opened the hat-box a little sea struck our bow with great violence and ran right up the jib. It was clear that there was no time for refreshment, and the hat-box was left half open and forgotten. "Luff her up," said Doe; "we'd better get near half-way to Hurst and then run across with a free sheet."

By this time the wind was blowing with gale force, and heavy rain made it as dark as pitch; but we had a little compass in a binnacle, and knew the course we were steering. After about a quarter of an hour or twenty minutes, on a west-south-westerly course, Doe said: "Now, sir, we'd better go for it; but as you be steering, get her clear of Fiddler's Race." I said: "All right, you tell me where it is when we get there."

Now Fiddler's Race is rather a remarkable little turmoil of waters. Even in comparatively calm weather, when wind and tide are in opposite directions, quite a serious little sea is knocked up, which may swamp an open boat. In a storm, steep, breaking seas, eight or ten feet high, make it a very dangerous place to approach. We must have made a record passage for a small sailing boat, from Hurst Bight towards Yarmouth. I have never been out in so violent a wind in an open boat. Half-way across, with big seas tumbling about on our starboard quarter, we saw the loom of Hurst Light, but could see nothing of Yarmouth. The problem was, where was Fiddler's Race? Was it to the right or to the left of our course?

We meant to leave it on our right, but had we perhaps been carried farther to the westward by the ebb tide? Ought we to bear away and make farther to the eastward? While we wondered, the problem was solved for us, and into the Race we went. There was no doubt about it, for a tidy sea came over the stern and filled us nearly full of water.

"Bail 'er, for God's sake!" shouts Doe, starting away at once with his bucket. I snatch my hat-box, the ideal bailer. Of course the first lot of water which I threw overboard took with it my top-hat, the whisky, the bread and butter, and the soda-water, but who cared? With feverish haste, steering with my back against the tiller, we both bailed at the maximum speed. One other sea we shipped, but we just kept her afloat until we ran into calmer water, and so into Yarmouth Harbour.

"That was a near thing," said Doe, after we had tied up to a barge, moored near the quay.

"Yes," I said. "I can never thank you enough for having got me across."

He said: "Don't you worry about that. I knew your Dad was that ill, you'd got to get across somehow."

So we tied up the boat as securely as we could, with fenders which we borrowed from the barge, to keep the two boats from grinding together too badly during the night. We also borrowed the barge's dinghy and got ashore.

A dogcart was waiting for me from my home at Brooke, and, with the aid of the coachman, we woke up a fisherman friend, who undertook to give a bed and warm clothes to gallant old Doe. Our coachman told me that my father was a little better, though dangerously ill. Still, there was time to get Doe a drink, and the inn provided me with hot water and rum, which I took across to Doe's kind host. Quickly we disposed of this warm drink. When I said to Doe: "Now, if I may, I will give you this fiver," he said, "No, sir, I won't have a penny." In vain did I implore him to accept the five-pound note. He absolutely refused, saying again and again: "I am not going to take money from a lad who is going to see his dying Dad." So I drove home in the dogcart, which was nearly blown right over more than once by the wind as we crossed an exposed part of the road, pondering deeply, as I still do, on the wonderful spirit of old Doe.

My father recovered, and lived for many years. With his

advice, I at last devised a form of present which Doe would accept.

One remarkable seaman whom I knew well from my earliest youth was Ben Jacobs, for thirty-seven years a member of our lifeboat crew, and for twenty-five years our coxswain. He died only four years ago, and all my life he was one of my greatest friends. He was more than six feet high, and of immense strength. His father, whom I just remember, was a tall man also. My father was fond of recalling the fact that old Jacobs, his two sons, Ben and Phil, and their sister, if laid down in line, stretched just over twenty-five feet.

Ben is a legendary hero in our village. One of my older friends said to me the other day: "Ben was as strong as a horse, braver than any lion, and gentle as a new-born lamb." This kindly son of Anak, for whom the sea had no terrors, had a most unexpected honour thrust upon him when the new Education Act was passed by Mr. Balfour's Government. In spite of his many great qualities of head and heart and muscle, he was a very poor hand at reading, and could hardly write at all. Under the new Act, it fell to the Isle of Wight County Council to appoint an Educational Representative to the Board of Management of our Elementary School. To their eternal honour, the Isle of Wight County Council appointed Ben. Of course, to the ordinary mind in England, it must have seemed a little odd that the man who was charged, with four others, with the task of supervising the education of the children should make his mark instead of signing his name, but the selection was wholly admirable and worked perfectly. Ben took immense pains in his new task. The children all adored him. When teaching them to play cricket, to row a boat, bait a line, spot a hare in its form—all the manifold things that he understood so well and of which he was a master—he would always add: "Now you pay attention to your schooling. I never had enough of it, and I've been sorry ever since."

He was the most skilful man in getting a boat off the beach in a rough sea that I have ever known. Single-handed he would run a fifteen-foot boat, stern on, as she had been left the night before, to the water's edge. With a swift movement he would spin her round with her bow pointing seaward. He would take one look to make sure that the tholepins were in place and the oars ready to his hands. Then he would grip the stern, and bending forward till his body was almost horizontal, he would push her out to sea. He would hold her for a moment when she was water-borne in a vice-like grip, keeping her bow pointing exactly to each oncoming wave, then, at what he adjudged to be the right moment—and he was rarely wrong—he would push her through the breaking wave, jump in over the stern, grab the oars, put them between the thole-pins, and standing up to his full height, push her with the weight of his whole body and his strong arms over the next wave and the next, and so out to sea. The combination of skill, nerve, and balance, was wonderful to behold.

I constantly went fishing with him, and often, with my other great friend, Tom Hookey, who succeeded Ben as coxswain of our lifeboat, we three made long trips together to the Needles, Christchurch, St. Catherine's, and sometimes far out to sea. But Ben's great qualities were devoted not only to his fishing and happy little adventures with me and Tom. His nerve and skill saved many lives from certain death by drowning. I used to remind him in his later years, to his great amusement, that we had one experience in common. We had both been first disgraced and then rewarded for the same action. During the South African War it fell to my lot to be placed under arrest for gross disobedience on active service, and eventually to receive the most coveted honour which can be bestowed on a soldier for the same act. In the same way, during the subsequent World War, my friend Ben was censured for failing in his duty, and then received the Silver Medal of the Royal National Lifeboat Institution for conspicuous courage on that same occasion. The censure was for not having observed a signal, a failure which might have resulted in the loss of life. The reward was for astonishing skill and courage in rescuing all the lives at hazard.

Rest to the soul of brave Ben Jacobs! He set an example of quiet good humour and dauntless courage to all of us here, which we pray we may be permitted to follow.

This is the kind of man you meet if you elect to take your holiday by sailing a boat, and so it seems to me that if any boy or man can choose the sport which will give him the most joy in life, I say, let him choose to sail a boat.

Reproduced from "For Ever England" (Hodder & Stoughton).

A House Set on a Hill

By Irene Prestwich

"This is the finest potato-growing land in Cheshire." The speaker was standing on a hillside that sloped to the sun and the south. The land was cropped with vegetables, and the owner had reason to be proud that the potatoes had not belied its reputation. For this was a private garden which had been famed for its beauty. Below stood Tirley, the grey-gabled house, overlooking one of the fairest views in Britain. Framed in a border of flowers like gay gems, its lawns and trees ran away into distant country. Beeston Castle on its rocky promontory stood up against the blue lines of the Peckfortons. It fronted the foothills of Wales, a bastion against the fierce hordes which used to raid the Cheshire plain. Chester Cathedral—gracious memorial to its founder, the saintly St. Werburgh—showed its square tower through a gap in the pine trees to the west.

What changes that hillside had seen! Once it had been part of Delamere Forest, hunting ground of William Rufus and a long line of kings. The forest on the northern slope of the hill and far beyond still belongs to the Crown. The owner of much of the neighbouring land proudly retains the title of King's Forester, and possesses the seven hundred year old horn which was the badge of that office.

The village of Utkinton at the foot of the slope straggles up the hill to the east, where each cottage garden has a view lovelier than the last. I remember how we talked of its ancient story with some of the villagers one winter evening. It was a strange January night, moonlit and warm. There was a sense of magic, of fairies and woodland folk around, that seemed to fill the air. Someone spoke of the supposed meaning of "Utkinton"—"outside the King's boundary"—a place of outlaws which our part of the forest had once been. It roused memories of the past in the village folk. One old man lived down a winding lane in a cottage that had been held rent free by his family for nearly a hundred years. His forefathers had won this privilege by clearing a stretch of forest land, building a house upon it, and undertaking to keep it cultivated.

The forest had had its footpads. It also had its healing waters: Wistlebitch well behind Hassall's farm at the crest of the hill. Here the country folk used to come by the hundred, and it was said not in vain, to find a cure for their ills. Further on in its green depths, at the end of a long winding path, you may find the strange hollow in the red sandstone rock known as the Urchin's Kitchen.

A crown of beech trees near the house marks the site of an ancient camp—the High Billinge—highest point in Cheshire, known and blessed by many a weary hunting man as he steered his way home by it in gathering dusk. For Tirley looks out on a country famous for long runs across country over stiff fences. It is within earshot of the chime of bells from fifteenth century Tarporley Church, and Tarporley was the centre of the Cheshire Hunt. There you may visit the Swan Inn and be shown the names and portraits of the Masters in the old ballroom, the scene until recent years of the Hunt Ball and the lively dinners of the Green Collar Club.

The site for this country house was originally bought by a business man from a neighbouring landowner. Architect and owner planned and built together in a riot of delight. Four-square round an inner court, with gabled roof and mullioned windows, it was worthy of the beauty of the countryside over which it seemed to watch. The design was at once delicate and massive.

On moonlit nights, when the tower and high west wing stood out in black shadow, it had the charm and mystery of an ancient castle. The hall, supported by great rafters, with its fine gallery and oriel window, was reminiscent of Elizabethan days. The long corridors, beautiful with repeating arches or crossbeams of oak, looked on to the inner court where, instead of an old well, a fountain played into a basin of blue mosaic.

For one reason or another neither its first nor its second owner was able to finish the house. It had passed into the hands of a neighbouring firm from whom my father, a business man from one of the manufacturing cities of the North, rented it two years before the first great war. For years the architect had waited while its fate hung in the balance. Now was his chance! He rushed home from abroad, delighted to find a family in sympathy with his conception. Together we began to plan and work to make a perfect whole of house and garden. Oak floors were laid down and planed with meticulous care. Details of wood and stone carving, plaster casts for ceilings, crystal candelabra and door handles, trails of vine up a leaded spout, the coloured lamp in the cloisters—nothing was too small for the architect's loving care, nothing was allowed to stand out obtrusively from the whole.

The garden, already partly planned as the setting for the house, began to grow alongside it: the terrace with formal beds, the wide herbaceous borders where hollyhocks were to make so exquisite a foreground to the blue hills. Across the smooth lawns were planted groups of crimson and pink and purple rhododendrons. A golden laburnum hung over a rock garden full of starry gems. A fan-shaped rose garden, surrounded with clipped yew hedges, ran down to the stream, and widened here and there into pools of water-lilies. The formal orchard had its showers of white and pink blossom, and every kind of flowering tree broke into bloom in the spring.

As the garden grew in beauty many people journeyed to see it and, though the rest of the family did not always feel so kindly, they were never too many for my father, who loved to have people about him. He would go out and meet them and chat in his simple, friendly way, delighted when they enjoyed what was such a pride and joy to him. People and societies of all kinds would send a polite little request "to see your lovely garden," and they were never refused.

We were a quiet family, accustomed to the life of a busy manufacturing town where people were simple and hospitable,

M

and where qualities of character and artistic achievement were reckoned on the whole above wealth or position. The move to the country was a great change. It was new and alluring to explore its beauty, to ride and walk in the forest and follow the hounds. People were friendly and curious, and called and asked us out. We went to tennis parties and country fêtes and race meetings. We basked in lovely houses and gardens. One was almost deluded into thinking that to live in a large house in the country was the answer to life, that it might satisfy with its beauty and pleasantness. But like many others in Britain we were blind to the forces that were shaping events. Our world ended with a crash on August 4th, 1914, two years after we came to Tirley.

To work hard and live away from home under war-time conditions was a new and deepening experience, and when the war ended it was not easy to take up again the life that was only really beginning in 1914. There was still the country to explore; there were hunting, bridge, golf and tennis. Occasionally the panelled hall would be cleared of its furniture for a dance, and the lights and flowers, the gay frocks and pink coats made a lovely scene. But it seemed to have lost something of its freshness and flavour. Perhaps the taint of disillusionment began to cast its blight over the effort to return to the good old days; or was it that the sacrifice of the war had awakened a "hunger for great living"—for a purpose in life that was worth giving everything for?

It might have been this which stirred a restless longing in my sister and me as we sat with my mother and father round the fire in the hall on winter evenings. Everyone thought of us as a happy family, surrounded by all we could want, yet even the perfection of the garden and the lovely country had a palling effect at times which I could not understand.

My mother found something satisfying in the way she cared for the home and garden and for our village neighbours. She was like the wife and mother in Proverbs 31, "whose price is far above rubies," "who worked willingly with her hands, stretched forth her hands to the poor, opened her mouth with wisdom, and in her tongue was the law of kindness." The neighbours began to turn to her, and she shared with them her skill in home crafts and handiwork. Her name is a household word to-day, loved by many whose homes we began to know.

By the time of the second great war my parents had both passed on, leaving behind the house and garden they had created, and a legacy of high character and honest dealing.

What was to become of Tirley?

It was much too big for my sister and me to live in. Would it be requisitioned by the Army? Used as an Institution? Become derelict? *Or was there a new use for country houses?*

During the uneasy years of peace between the two wars I had come across a group of people who were unlike any I had met before, people who were determined to build a world that works, a world built on sacrifice, sound living and hard thinking. It did not take very long to decide that here was a purpose satisfying yet ever-unfolding. Dreams of what a large country home could do that was used for such a purpose began to possess me, and at last the time came when they could be fulfilled. It was the moment just before Dunkirk, when the fall of France was imminent and the country was faced with one of the worst crises in its history. At this time large-scale evacuation from London was being urged in the national interest. I decided to offer Tirley as an emergency headquarters for Moral Re-Armament to whom I owed this new conception of living, for while their London headquarters must be continuously manned, much of the work could be carried on from blitz-free Cheshire. My offer was accepted. Soon, typewriters, files and furniture began to move in, and with them some of the gayest, hardest working people I have ever met. None of us then could foresee the opportunities that would open out. The traditions of the old home remained—the foundations had been well and truly laid. It was still a home and a family, but now it was to be a family whose responsibilities stretched far beyond the confines of a home, to the nation, the Empire, a new world.

The new household grew daily. The old family of four had been waited on by a staff of nine maids and a housekeeper. I, who had scarcely been allowed to put coal on the fire, now found myself scrubbing potatoes for forty people and enjoying it. Other women of my age, mothers whose families had grown up, women who had loved their own homes, came to help in the work of the kitchen and house. They shared their skill and knowledge in home crafts, cooking, bottling, thinking and caring for the visitors, arranging beds, mending linen, giving the touches that made Tirley more of a home than ever. "And we get on," said one of them to a young American officer who was having lunch there one day. "Well," he replied, "if fifteen of you older women can live in one house and get on together, you've sure got something to tell the world." But it was more than learning how to get on together. They had an answer for the broken marriages, the slipping standards, the lax discipline that were undermining the moral fibre of the nation. They had come determined to fight for home life with all that the word implies of high standards, faith in God, and service to the community, and this did not admit of any sitting back at an age when most people feel they can claim an easier life.

Ethel, the maid who came daily from the village, found life a new adventure as she worked in the scullery those days. It might be a General from India or a labourer from the docks who wiped the dishes as she washed up at the sink. Or it might be John, who was often at Tirley and took his share in the running of the house. John is the Director and Manager of one of the largest tanneries in the North of England. He said: "It was in the scullery at Tirley that I learned to work as a team with anyone, and I was able to take that spirit back to my own work." John had distrusted his shop steward. He thought he was the cause of all the trouble at the works. But he found at Tirley that "Honest apology starts team work." He tried it out, and it brought a new confidence between them. In fact, it began a new era for the tannery. "There is no problem," said the shop steward and foreman when they visited Tirley one day, "that the three of us together cannot solve unitedly."

But the greatest activity centred on the gardens, which were mobilized for food production. Tennis courts, lawns, and meadows were all ploughed up. Bronze-leaved beetroot took the place of wallflowers in the box-edged beds on the terrace. In the national emergency I decided to run the estate as a market garden, and seven girls volunteered to take it on with me. None of them had any previous experience of land work. The day the ploughing began I asked the Scottish head gardener, who had been at Tirley over a quarter of a century, if he felt sad. "Sad? No, Miss—why, the land will be *producing* now!"

It was a hard battle, but a repaying one. The girls discovered that the yearly trenching of the circular kitchen garden was a highly skilled art. They found the zest of digging in a winter dawn; the triumph of seeing, at the end of a hot day, the young plants blue-green against the freshly-hoed earth. Someone asked the head gardener what it was like having seven land-girls instead of a dozen men. "I'd rather have these girls than any of them." "Why?" "They never need telling twice—and they never look at the clock."

"Perfect work first time" was one of the principles of the market garden. A six-horse-power tractor was delivered, demonstrated, and then left for Mary and Heather to master. Mary had never handled an engine before, and neither had done any ploughing. They tackled one of the tennis courts. The machine backed them into the walls and pushed them into the magnolias, yet at the end of the day a neighbouring farmer stared at the straight furrows. "Well," he said, as he scratched his head, "that ploughing was never done by novices."

The first year was a stiff fight against weeds and inexperience, a fight in which character was grown as well as crops. At the end of the second year a member of the War Agricultural Executive Committee said, "There has been a hundred per cent. improvement. If you go on like this you'll be teaching us farmers something."

Each girl's work produced enough vegetables to feed fifty people every day in the year. One of the tennis courts alone produced 5,000 lettuces followed by 7,000 leeks in one season. Miners, school teachers, service men, dockers, and children all helped during their holidays in rush marketing and planting-out periods. Among them was Geoffrey, brother of one of the land girls. He was a Commando officer, who won the D.S.O. and the M.C. and bar, and later gave his life in the invasion of Sicily. "The spirit and training I get here," he said, "is just what I need."

I knew the satisfaction of the garden in the old days with its perfectly-kept lawns and borders. But it was as nothing to the satisfaction of seeing a loaded van ready for market. The decision to sell only when vegetables were at their best did not always mean top prices, but it meant a sure market for goods that were always sound. A dealer in Liverpool who handles thousands of tons of potatoes in the year said, "Those potatoes of yours were first rate. I took a bag home for my family."

The Harvest Home was a great occasion, when a hundred and forty sat down to a rabbit pie supper in the hall. All our friends were there—farmers, local craftsmen and retailers from

Chester. One of the War Agricultural Committee officials said, "In the spirit you have here at Tirley I see hope for the future of agriculture."

Perhaps there was a secret at Tirley that had grown under the stone roof as it took on the colour of the countryside. One spring in this hillside garden, when the blossom was out and the land furrowed under the plough, someone wrote:

> April came with a warm June sun,
> Blossom of pear and plum
> Rose-pearl of apple-blossom
> Rioted over the earth:
> Promise of spring,
> Of hearts blossoming,
> Over the ploughed red earth.
>
> So fair was the earth this year,
> Colour on colour laid,
> Spring's bronze and green and gold
> In the blue hills disappear,
> Wealth of His world untold
> Waiting the consummation
> Of God's purpose in creation
> One-ness with Him, with man,
> And the beauty that He hath made.

This secret might have accounted for the change in the views of a young pacifist who spent one Christmas there, for he decided to go into the Army and later won the M.C. He had spent the holiday making a beautiful crib with thatched roof. There it stood at the foot of the great tree in the hall, the light of a candle thrown on the group of shepherds and kings round Mother and Child. The tree looked down on the family below and seemed to breathe a sheltering peace. The carol-singing and living silences spoke to the heart, and were long remembered by those who experienced them.

One Christmas a Bishop from the Far East, who was staying with us, told stories of a new spirit in Burma. Somehow the problems of relationships, the seemingly insoluble problem of Empire, began to melt away as he talked. An Indian officer, listening to the Bishop's stories, was disarmed by his willingness to shoulder his own country's mistakes, and began to find a new love for Britain. "I have seen something to-night," he said, "that has made me want to give my life to make Britain great."

It was a supernational gathering that Christmas, made up of many from different parts of the world: Louis, Town Clerk and golden singer from Jamaica, finding an answer for the coloured races; Gerry, a naval commander recently returned from an important mission in North Africa; Andrew, repatriated prisoner of war, who had fought for and maintained a high morale in his prison camp; Philippe and Helène, the young Swiss diplomat and his wife, who had seen the same spirit of Moral Re-Armament at work, on a recent visit to America, reconciling warring factions in industry, and were convinced that here was the only thing that could bring renaissance to Europe.

Many others from America visited us. It was a historic day when Mike, old friend but young Lieutenant, brought his Colonel to Tirley. The welcome sign and the flags were out at the front door—the Union Jack on one side, a gold-fringed Stars and Stripes on the other. Then there was that other Colonel from Texas, Bob, superb horseman and loved friend wherever he went. Bob had the gift of investing his friends and every situation with greatness. Whether by some thoughtful kindness, or some special job he had for you, he possessed the art of winning people, of getting them to do the unexpected thing. Later we heard that he had been honoured with one of the highest awards in the United States Army, the Legion of Merit, for signal service in the defence of London against the V-bombs. Bob wrote to us: "I love your great country more than I can say," and we, who valued his friendship, were proud to have been able to forge one more of those indissoluble links between our two countries.

So Tirley thinks gratefully of all the friends whom it has welcomed from across the world: of François and Maurice, who symbolize the new spirit rising in France; of Aagot, whose home in Norway was a fortress of resistance against Nazism; of Jim and Gordon from Australia, who helped to clear the seas for D-Day; of Tom from Ireland, who gave his life at Alamein; and a host of others from every continent who go marching through our hearts as we look forward hopefully to the future.

Tirley has weathered two wars with an unbroken record as a home. What part will homes play in shaping a lasting peace? Is there a new spirit stirring them, the spirit of those who fought and died to preserve our Christian heritage? We believe there is, and that the experience of these years has taught us to value that heritage afresh. It has aroused in us the determination to fight for it as the one enduring strength of the nation.

Time and the Welsh Mountains

By Rhys Davies

THE overburdened little bus staggers up hills and gallops down slopes as gallantly as one of those native mountain ponies it has, alas! almost banished from these antique roads. Panting, it drops me at the inn, where I leave my bag for collection by the farm cart in the morning, and jolts on with its crowd of loquacious alert-eyed people babbling excitedly in that language which, even more than the faces and vivacity of the people, makes England seem very far away. I like arriving at dusk in this village in the heart of Wales. It is not a 'pretty' village; few Welsh villages have that rustic charm favoured by manufacturers of calendars and picture postcards. Its street is angular, grey, slate-roofed, with the nonconformist chapel striking a (deceptively) bleak note, and the inn is grimly independent of extraneous lure.

But it lies in a graceful water-blue hollow streaked by hillstreams. In the mild sheltered air I can hear the energetic canticles of those pure waters; a music everlasting as the distant mountains from where these streams issue and which has affinities with those melodious voices in the bus. As I climb a road above the main stream I can see, in the small whitewashed farmhouses and cottages scattered on slopes, tilting pastures and knolls of autumnal purple, lamp after lamp suddenly gleam out. They give me a sense (again, sometimes deceptive) of domestic twilight repose and serene remoteness from what is called the world. There is a smell of moist green cresses, damp roots, and a watered earth that yet keeps brisk with sunshine. And, as always in Wales, there is a sense of mountains not far off. Old, old mountains.

Climbing the rutted road, that *odour*, as it were, of the mountains reaches into my very being. And I think how it has been the dominant flavour of Wales. For one native historian Wales' mountains explain the nation's isolation and independence (the people, of course, have never been conquered by England); but also: "The wild and rugged outlines of the mountains are mirrored as intense but broken purposes in the Welshman's character, always forming great ideals but lacking in the steady perseverance of the people of the plain. The mountains, his mute but suggestive companions, strengthen his imagination. His imagination makes him exceedingly impressionable—he has always loved poetry and theology; but this very imagination, while enabling him to see great ideals, makes him incapable of realizing them."

Whatever their social and spiritual influence has been, they certainly give to Wales a look of being enclosed eternally in its own richness. Even in this district, where what properly can be termed mountains lie in distant abeyance, I can sense them through the dusk. But on a clear day I can see their dramatic contours, apple-green, citron-veined and with delicate lilac shadows. They look as if they had been dropped that very morning from the fresh heavens. Yet how old with history are these mountains, how stained with the blood of their antique defenders. And there is a kind of biblical prestige about them. They seem, so to speak, pieces of the world's original furniture;

they arrived from the hand of the Great Craftsman at the best period.

More lamps appear in the far distances, in the remote secret folds, *cwms* and exposed eminences. At last the lamps again, to welcome the traveller! Soon perhaps the yellow butter, pale cheeses and silvery pink hams which once overflowed from the cornucopia of this district will appear in civilized plenty again. I know each of the white houses, some intimately, others by repute. They are nearly all farmhouses, in this land of tiny farms worked usually by members of the family alone. My relative, at whose farm I am arriving, will have six months of local happenings waiting for recital to me. I imagine her airing at this very moment the flannel night-shirt I always borrow on the first night of my visits. It belongs to her son, not demobilized yet from the Navy, and before that it belonged to her eldest brother, now dead. Woven of Welsh mountain-sheep wool, with an old tenacity in the weaving, I feel it is likely to be worn by generations as yet unborn. I consider these solid flannel shrouds to be unhygienic and a dangerous habit, but Rhoda will have none of my finicky modern ideas.

Arosfa is the name of the farm she and her husband run. I think of the other beautiful names in this district—Nantcellan, Frondolau, Derwyn Llas, Lechryd, Erw-isaf; they, too, have something of the streams' music. They belong to a language that sprang from the touch, movements and sounds of nature. Arosfa stands on the shoulder of a ravine; there is the scent of pines. It is one of the smallest of the local farms. Howell, my relative by marriage, finds time to be the district's grave-digger. He is not at home when I arrive. Rhoda, his wife, turns up the lamp's wick as high as it will go. And Erasmus, the real autocrat of the house, wrapped in his shawls by the fireside, casts on me one half challenging, half jesting eye—the other one appears to be wholly and slyly calculating. Known as Erasmus Aberyst-wyth (his proper surname is Jones), he is a very distant relative and an immovable non-paying lodger, a man of obscure physical ailments and scholarly hobbies.

Rhoda automatically turns the airing nightshirt; a chicken boils in the deep fireplace alcove. She is tall and robust, rust-coloured; her walk has a slow straight grace and, unlike the vivacious ebullience of most of her race, she thinks and speaks slowly, feeling out into the world with caution. But she assesses everything and everyone with a sure if ponderous honesty; she is a true daughter of the mountains. Her immediate concern is with food, the comfort of my bed, and the fact that facial pallor is a matter for dire gloom. For her, towns are Babylons. Margarine and dried egg Babylons, I think.

"Everyone," wheezes Erasmus cantankerously, "can't live top of a pine wood and get blown inside out in the winds up here."

He has now got rheumatism. By an insidious system of complaining and criticism Erasmus has attained to high and solid status in the household. Except to go to the earth-closet—a trip involving extra shawls, an old square bowler hat, and a walking-stick—he rarely leaves the house. His corner by the fireplace is the cosiest in the room, the armchair belongs to him alone. He has lived there for fifteen years on the proceeds, as it were, of two important happenings—breaking his leg and winning an Eisteddfod prize of five pounds for a Welsh essay. Both of these events took place in Aberystwyth, where he lived then.

At that period, determined to learn the English language properly, he used to study a dictionary in bed (after various brief jobs, he had become an auctioneer). One afternoon he sat downstairs in his lodging laboriously composing a letter in English; he went upstairs to fetch the dictionary and, intently looking up the word 'exhibition' as he ambled along the landing, he missed the top stair and fell headlong. From the hospital he got in touch with Rhoda. She, a woman with a deep elemental compassion in her soul, decided that besides breaking his leg the fall might affect his mind. He had already won that prize at an Eisteddfod and thereby earned distinction and that great respect for things to do with the Word which is so firmly, and rightly, ingrained in the Welsh. But Erasmus' landlady in Aberystwyth did not want him back.

So he moved to Arosfa, vaguely for convalescence, but really for ever. Unmarried and with no money, stout but peevish, thereafter he devoted himself to armchair scholarship, argument and the cultivation of ailments. Sometimes he did some cooking for Rhoda from the chair, a frying pan in one hand, a book in the other. Her husband accepted him with a polite resignation in keeping with his Christian character; he also had respect for scholarly attainments, and Erasmus had taught much of the

English language to the son, Morgan, who now often wrote letters home in English.

Presently Howell looms into the lamplight's soft yellow throw. He had entered the house silently. There is always something of the noiseless waverings of smoke in his movements. He is a lean, lightly-stepping man with a sinewy face and hands of taut strength. His keen bare-looking nose, black hair and bright black eyes seem very Welsh; he is of the long-skulled Iberian type. His blue-eyed wife with her heavier mould and her tendency to a reddish blondness is of the later Celtic stock; she does not possess the satiric humour, sly and intelligent, of her husband; she is more the misty dreamer of Merlin's domain. Erasmus seems to be a crossing of these two types; his rather sensual physical presence is redeemed by his scholarship.

It is in such isolated districts as this, protected by mountains, that the pure racial types are found untarnished by time. Now and again, with a start of recognition, one comes across them in the industrial parts of Wales, but there they have an accidental and almost alien look. Close-packed communal living tends, through the generations, to obliterate the original hallmarks and to produce imitative types belonging solely to the coal-pits, the ironfields and the factories. Sometimes I have sat in houses of this pastoral district and, listening to the antique language and watching the vivid play of expression on these cleanly pure faces, felt time abolished. It was that very day the Roman legions left the fringes of this Western land with its strange magic green like the green in a cat's eye. The passing of the centuries is an illusion; Owain Glyndwr is still in the mountains and the alien English soldiers still affrighted by this wild land, with its witch's brew of sudden storms, and by this battling with a magician who consorted with anti-English "spirits of the vasty deep."

Howell asks Erasmus if he collected the acorns at the bottom of the ravine, for the pigs. It seemed, marvellously, that he had undertaken to accomplish this task; there were great quantities this year. Erasmus shook his head and began to groan about his autumnal rheumatism coming back and stabbing him 'like a carving knife.' Howell winked his black eye at me and Erasmus said with testy haughtiness, "No need to wink, Howell. Rhoda had to rub that liniment on me."

Rhoda said deprecatingly, " 'Rasmus couldn't bend all that

time picking up a lot of old acorns." She profoundly understood his lack of need to bestir himself from the precincts of the house; it would be a colossal upheaval for him to go so far—a quarter of a mile.

Once, a few years ago, I succeeded in persuading Rhoda to take a twenty-mile bus ride with me to a seaside town. Her preparations for this were careful and involved. Finery I had never seen appeared out of old chests; though it was summer I was told she was wearing extra things against draughts. She looked handsome and very settled in her fifty years of excellent health. During the bus ride she wore a serious, watchful but unyielding expression. In the town she pondered over a draper's window and begged me to go in with her to buy a corset. (A shop on wheels called at the farm twice a month, its owner an intimate friend of all the local families.) Her preliminary scrutiny of the saleswoman here was shrewd, and when she prepared to pay she brought out from some secret place in her clothes a thick wad of notes, at least fifty pounds. I asked her why she had brought so much money, but she shook her head very mysteriously; I think she felt that terrible things might happen to her in the town and only money could save her. But it was in a restaurant that her suspicions were most pronounced; she refused to eat the beef and produced from her bag a glass jar of her own butter and slices of boiled ham. Her scrutiny of the townspeople had a prudent but astonished intensity; soon a high colour began to burn in her cheeks. She pretended she hadn't seen the women bathers walking in their abbreviated costumes into the sea. In the cinema she sat in a sort of startled depression. I could get no comments from her.

But that night, though safely back in her own bed, she gave vent. The never-ill Rhoda was violently sick. Her husband running for a pan, Erasmus heaved out of his slumbers and shouting dramatically, and myself feeling responsible, created a memorable occasion talked of to this day.

She dishes up the boiled chicken; it is a special treat for me after my enormous sixty-mile journey, and not their usual supper fare—her own delicious bread, butter and cheese. Erasmus has written a hymn since my last visit; she asks him to show it to me, and her manner pronounces that a man who writes a hymn has no need to go collecting acorns. Howell has been digging a grave that afternoon; he receives seven-and-six

for this. There is still about him a slight odour of rich clay.
His tankard of beer laced with a drop of whisky is warming
on the hearth. The two household books stand together as
always on the mantelpiece—a Welsh Bible and a stout illus-
trated compilation called "Your Body and its Care."

The daughter of a neighbour farmer is getting married.
Rhoda gravely shows me the presents for her: a stuffed stag's
head (from Howell) and a young aspidistra in a painted pot
(from Rhoda). The stag's head has hung in the barn for years,
but Howell has freshened it and polished the eyes. The painted
pot is hideous. But I sit and wonder at the primitive natural
poetry lurking about Rhoda as she delicately and tenderly
touches the leaves of the aspidistra, whereas the sumptuous
pageant of wild outdoor plants and trees she was bred amongst
does not rouse interest in her. I resolve to bring her one of
those writhen eccentric-looking potted cactus some day. She
will think more of it than of the wonderful chestnut tree
shading the house.

The honeymoon is to be spent in Aberystwyth. "They will
have rough seas there next month," Erasmus observes with
satisfaction. "The sea comes over from America full pelt in
November." This leads him into reminiscences of some of the
awful marine upheavals he witnessed in his auctioneering days,
and yet again he tells me of that local custom (in the very old
days) when the fishermen tried to placate the stormy waters
by taking a chapel preacher down to the sea on a Sabbath and
dipping him in. This apparently true story always rouses Rhoda
to indignation—what, let a preacher risk catching pneumonia
for the sake of a few fish! She is not at all roused against the
superstition of this attempt to mollify a dim but angry Neptune.
In her bones she is aware of the religious awe which prompted it.

As I lie in bed I can see an enormous star through the open
window. It flashes in nakedly like the terrible blue eye of a god.
As always, I feel in the night of this land a living sense of an
antiquity that has not changed. The silence is freshly alive, and
it is not like the cessation of activities which is the silence of
a town. There is no haste in this place, no consciousness of the
hurrying years; the closing of day, the arrival of morning do
not seem directed by man and his habits. Here the living clarity
of that star has a watchful contact with the earth. I sink refreshed
into sleep.

On Sunday I go with Rhoda and Howell to Soar, the 'independent' chapel (Capel y Annibynnwr) in the village. Erasmus stays at home, shawled and artfully expressing envy. He expects the chapel to be brought to him, in the shape of the minister, who, however, does not care for a theological conference with him. It is a fine golden day. Sheep, those chief treasures of the Welsh farmer with their tough wool but tender flesh, dot the placid green slopes. In the village people have an air of bustling importantly to chapel; even the streams seem to run faster. But the inn is resolutely closed for the day. A white goat with a whiter kid munches bushes in the chapel yard; a deacon with a hostile face drives them out. There goes little Jenkin Williams, trotting in with his mother. Last year this boy of nine had made a sudden comment on the selfish habit, in the monthly communion services, of grown-ups taking a piece of bread off the silver dish passed round the pews but leaving him severely alone. One Sunday after the plate had yet again passed him by, he took a crust of his mother's home-made bread out of his pocket and began to eat it.

The atmosphere in the plain little chapel is one of pleasure. Darting glances note every entrance, and if there is a solemn air of starched-collars, Sabbath finery and moth-balls, human warmth predominates. This is the weekly gathering of a people for the most part scattered among lonely hills. The remote kind of life led in the old days, when communications were few, bred a great need for human society in this imaginative race. The Nonconformist movement, with its first itinerant preachers penetrating determinedly into lonely folds and more domestic in their appeal than the priests of the proud Established Church, performed a great work in uniting the people socially. When the chapels were built there was quick and ready support for them. To-day the weekly service is still as much an enthusiastic social event as an act of worship. Even the most wordly and successful resident, the big cattle-dealer who has built himself an imitation-English 'villa' and who is the one local man to acquire real wealth, still remains faithful to the chapel of his fathers—and despite the chronic drinking habit riches have brought. He will still brag to you of the day many, many years ago when, a boy of seventeen, he invested all his widowed mother's capital in one black bullock and took it to market from their mud-walled cottage. His befeathered, spick-and-span wife sits beside him in a specially cushioned pew; she has the look of a woman who fumes a great deal.

The minister is one of the last of the old hierarchy of dramatic preachers. After the full-bodied singing he rises with an authoritative dignity to give the sermon, and, like the artist he is, he begins austerely, reserving his full powers for that rhetorical display which will precede the last hushed moments, the classic 'dying fall.' If analysed, the subject and words of his sermon would seem trite; all is in the manner of delivery. He has a beautiful voice, an eye of fine frenzy, and the hypnotic magic of the born actor. I have seen him crowd the pulpit vividly with all the creatures of Noah's Ark and bring down a dove so realistically out of the chapel's rafters that one could hear the flutter of its wings. At last he mounts into the *hwyl*, the incantory singing which moves from a sort of primitive wail to the pæan of an anthem. *Hwyl* is really a tonal play on a simple phrase arriving in the sermon and sometimes its one jewel. To-day this phrase is: "They shall go down into the dark places, but they shall see the stars." The lamenting starts with the word 'down' which is repeated groaningly and with such gestures that flights of evil dark stairs leading to abysmal horrors appear before one. He stares earthwards, he shudders, his voice tolls funereal bells. . . . But the stars, the stars, the stars! His arms are thrown out, his eyes scan the heavens, his voice mounts and mounts. The stars! He does not say so, but in that visionary moment the stars leap back and the holy cherubim appear before the terrific Throne of flame and marble. He allows the dazzling vision to appear for just the right fraction of time, and, dropping his arms, his voice descends to the peaceful close.

Throughout the sermon subdued cries of agreement and appreciation are heard from the congregation and the row of deacons under the pulpit. Otherwise all is hushed, with the deep hush of a tranquil pleasure. There is also a feeling of life's fret and worries set at naught. The concluding hymn has the surge of refreshment. From remote fields, old uplands and windy hillsides people hardily occupied with the biological facts of cattle and the productivity of solid earth have met together in acknowledgment of their deepest needs, and they are not going away famished.

In the lobby, on the porch-steps, and in the yard they greet

N

each other with animated satisfaction. As a non-resident I am given special attention. I have come from a 'foreign' world and, despite many visits and the family roots in the district, I am still examined carefully for a sign of oddness. These real country people (in Wales there is still very little evidence of the mongrel kind of ruralism) are, thank heaven, not a whit aware that in a uniform world of mass-production, rational education and mechanical triumphs it is they who retain the primeval individuality of character. They draw disposition and temper from the original breathing earth, as the townsman draws his from sleek tarmac, cindery rail-tracks and mathematical pavements.

Olwen, a farmer's daughter, healthy as a bounding wind, challenges me once more with her taunts and her swinging, blackly jeering eyes. What, not yet married! Well, Joanna is still waiting for me. (This Joanna is a repellent 'pig woman' living alone in a filthy hovel.) All persons who have not undertaken the chapel marriage ceremony are subject unweariedly to this form of bucolic humour. I assume it springs from an old tribal instinct against the critic of domestic custom, *i.e.*, mock the outlaw into obedience. Olwen is joined by a girl friend who increases the battery. It seems that Joanna is in such a state of doleful pining that her pig-sty hasn't been cleaned for weeks. There is no cruelty in their fun about the awful Joanna; she is a twist of nature they accept in unsentimental simplicity. Olwen's splendid hips move harmoniously as a circling young mare's flanks. Her creamy throat gurgles like a dove's. But she has, too, a fine haughtiness. It is displayed unconsciously against persons like myself who have made the transition from the ancestral pastoral life to town life. She is not *consciously* aware that she possesses a great pride in the old tradition; but it all comes out subtly in her untrammelled glances, her bubbling if rude humour, and occasionally in a fine antique courtesy.

I must come over to her father's farm on Wednesday, to supper. She has thought out some new riddles for me (*i.e.*, a test of the intelligence of this townsman). Olwen's home is the only house I know where the old traditional riddle game is still an evening entertainment. In the past the riddles were asked in Welsh rhyme composed by local bards. A rough translation of one runs: "I have been a tear in the air, I have been the dullest of stars; I was made of the flower of nettles, and of the water of the ninth wave; I played in the twilight, I slept in purple; my fingers are long and white, it is long since I was a herdsman."

Olwen's riddles are by no means as mysterious as this. One of hers ran: "My mouth is black, I have four feet, my weight is a hand's weight, I take the brush, I like winter." The answer was a coal scuttle.

Presently these Sunday figures can be seen winding away into the different green fastnesses where the little sturdy white houses sit so comfortably. May this country never die, may it never be broken up by more of these appalling arterial roads, brazen 'holiday camps,' and the thing that asbestos huts, gun-sites and refugees symbolize. May that fallow field with its skimming birds, the pasture quiet with musing cattle, the moist hillside patched with sheep, remain unmolested. It is of course romantic to expect this countryside and these glimpses of the old life to remain unchanged. People are truly alive only by virtue of the pulse dominating the world—a pulse throbbing at present with strange new activities. Yet does the old poetry of earth change? Taliesin, an early Welsh visionary, said that 'man is oldest when he is born, and is younger and younger continually.' I like to think that this is a prophetic utterance about his race, which he knew would always concern itself chiefly with that enduring thing, the seasonal soil.

Olwen will travel in an aeroplane, and apparently she will adjust herself to whatever the 'atomic age' (one helplessly but suspiciously uses the newspaper term) will bring. But her children will surely possess the attributes of her race which she herself owns after many centuries of other marvellous changes. And chief of these is her unselfconscious kinship with this pastoral sanctuary protected by those encircling, ancient and ever-young mountains.

N*

"Cy"

By Walter Rose

Cy rang the bells of Aston Church. His full name was "Cyrus"; the village called him "Cy" for convenience.

They were deep-sounding bells—three in number—full-throated and sonorous. We boys mimicked their sound, that each Sunday morning came floating over the meadows. To us, they seemed to say "Lar, um, pom—Lar, um, pom." In some unexplained manner they were appropriate to the low-lying meads that enclosed that small village, comprising its church, a rectory, one large farm, and some half dozen cottages. Their voices seemed to be like the bellow of the large kine that grazed those meadows knee-deep in lush grass; they told of stability and the fat substance of life.

The road that led into the village came to a dead end just beyond the last cottage, where a field gate barred further advance to ordinary folk. Beyond the gate spread broad open meadows, in which cattle grazed for weeks on end without seeing a stranger. Rights of way over them existed, available to the few who happened to know them. They led to no place of importance, so were rarely used; so seldom that no track was visible. Those, who by chance did go, took their bearings from known trees, or gates, in the distance, anon pausing to ensure that they were proceeding in the right direction.

In that small backwater of civilization, Cy had lived the whole of his life. From boyhood onward he had always worked on its one large farm and rarely did he go beyond the parish. He asked of life nothing beyond the simple routine of the village, its doings for many years past were chronicled in his mind; the rectors who had come and gone, the births and deaths, in addition to a multitude of minor happenings on the farm, where he had witnessed the continual displacement of labour by machinery.

No one disliked Cy. In fact the village was very fond of him. His features were grotesque to the extent that no lass had ever encouraged his advances, yet they represented only benevolence and kindness, the spirit of his contentment. His face was about as wide as it was high; the hair of his head left only a narrow strip of forehead above his eyebrows, while both nose and mouth were excessive in width. Yet in his eyes a cheerful twinkle lurked and a permanent hollow, like an elongated dimple abode at each end of his over-extended mouth. When spoken to, the dimple began to quiver, the eyelids to take on strange shapes, while the eyes expressed the geniality of his simple heart.

He did the menial work of the farm, the cleaning out of the pig sties, and cowhouses, and the sodden ditches of the wide meadows. There at times he worked for days on end, where, from morn till eve, no man passed, his boots and gaiters laden with the sticky soil. There he ruminated on the small happenings of the village; the crops in the cottage gardens and the fields; the horses, the sheep and the cattle; the period of the year and the condition of the weather. In all these he felt himself in real unity with the rest of the village, the crowning glory being the knowledge that he, alone, rang the bells of its church each Sunday.

His fellow-workers—as such men always do—understood his mentality, and when in distant fields, on seeing the squat tower amid the elms they would exclaim, "There's the old church, Cy. Come Sunday you'll be on again." Cy's face never failed to glow with enthusiasm at the remark, and his deep-chested reply never varied. "Aye, I'll make um rattle."

To ring those heavy bells, in correct rotation, involved no mean skill. Cy, though unable to explain the method to another, had done it for so long and so often that to him it was simplicity itself. The rope of a bell in each hand and his foot in a noose at the end of the rope of the third, in that manner he rang them correctly and with good volume of sound.

Each Sunday they vied with the bells of the next parish, also three in number. These were of lighter sound and seemed to denote its squire, with his lady, in church parade, walking their private way to the church and followed by their sons and daughters in couples, the footman and butler in livery and, lastly, the serving maids. Each of those trios sounded in competition with the full peal of eight of much lighter tone, from the tower of my native village; also, according to the way of the wind, with the fainter sounds of bells of parishes further away.

It was in this combined oblation of sound that Cy experienced his soul's real satisfaction. There, at the end of that small church, beneath the cross beams that supported the belfry above, his body swayed to and fro to the rhythm of movement and melody of noise. He heard it overhead, the strong metallic strike of each clapper precise to time; he heard the sounds chasing and vibrating round the church, the deep full notes echoing and re-echoing—a delirious intermingled hum of which he, himself, was the soul and centre. He knew that it was heard all over the small village, also, afar, over the fields where he had worked during the week; that folk, hearing it, would know that it was time to don their Sunday best and make for church.

If they were late, it was not Cy's fault. He had his trusty watch, which hung on the church wall, on a nail he had driven for that express purpose. It was his most cherished possession, the gift of a former rector, who had become very fond of him. He carried it in a secret pocket, inside the top of his cord trousers; there he could feel its comforting shape and, at times, imagine that he felt the vibration of its tick. It hung at the head of his bed, its ticking often the only sound throughout the long night.

The gift of the watch established his position as unofficial time-keeper to the village. Thereafter, if anyone needed to know the hour he was advised to ask Cy. His watch could be trusted, for he confirmed it each day by the postman, who had become so familiar with the request as not to wait to be asked.

The watch, to Cy, was a marvellous work of art. It belonged to a realm of ideas and skill far beyond his own life. Tenderly he would hold it in his hand and watch the small seconds hand complete the circuit of its small dial, responsive to each tick. He had been cautioned against opening the interior, yet, at times, the temptation was irresistible. Over the escape wheel was a gleaming shape of metal that shone like gold; it was chased with flowing lines of decorative foliage. The click that sounded as he closed it never failed to thrill him.

Each night he wound it slowly and with care. The rector had explained the delicacy of the operation and Cy's reverence for the watch was too great for him to disregard it. The chain that preserved it from theft, or fall, passed round his neck, from there in double lines travelled down his chest, finally reaching the watch, snugly reposing in its warm pocket. To raise it he pulled the chains upward with his left hand in readiness to secure it when it appeared.

Only once had it stopped; the event threw Cy's whole life into utter disorder. Folk asked him the time, he shook his head sadly and in distress produced the watch, which he had duly wound and carefully shaken, also opened and examined the motionless wheels, all to no purpose. They advised him to take it to a jeweller in the nearest market town. There, that same evening, he walked the full three miles, only to find that the shop had just closed. He hammered the door. He felt it to be a case of urgency and that folk should not shut their shops so early when matters of such moment required attention. Hearing the noise, the jeweller appeared from a side entrance. "What did he want?" Cy produced the watch. "It had stopped," he said gravely. "He had come to see if he would make it go again." With dread at heart he anxiously watched the jeweller deftly open it and give a cursory look at the works.

"All right. I'll see to it," said he.

"Not broke but what it can't be repaired?" asked Cy.

'Oh no," replied the jeweller. "Wants cleaning. Leave it to me. I'll put it right for you."

A look of intense relief spread over Cy's face. "And when will it be done, sir?" he asked.

"That's a question," said the jeweller shortly. "I'm full up with repairs." He paused. "Say a week from now."

Somewhat dismayed, Cy could but submit to the ruling of knowledge and ability. He reflected as he strode along the way to the village, that a Sunday would intervene. His only other timepiece was a thirty-hour grandfather in a painted deal case, which in a dusky corner of his living-room stood silent, its hands denoting a quarter to one. For years past its behaviour had been erratic, with the result that for long he had ceased trying to make it go. He knew full well that the whole village would wait for the bells to tell them when it was time to prepare for church; the full triple peal for twenty minutes, succeeded by the two smaller bells, each rung singly, for five minutes, called "the ten" and "the five."

It was Cy's insistence on time, and his trouble with his tall clock, that had prompted the rector's happy idea to give him the watch. Since then, through Cy, the village had conformed to its ruling—as folks are always ready to do when they have faith in a ruling's integrity. The dilemma occupied his thoughts all the way home; at night, afterwards in a silence made poignant by absence of the accustomed tick, he pondered on it. Throughout the days following he missed it sadly and found himself constantly feeling for it in the empty pocket. The hours of each day seemed to drag slowly. He did not realize that, in the matter of time, he had become mechanized. When in those distant meadows he reverted again to his primary instincts and watched the position of the sun, the lengthening of the tree shadows, the density of the atmosphere and the return of the rooks to their communal roosting place. Yet, in that manner, he judged, fairly correctly, the time to cease work and return to his cottage home.

On Sunday, his employer—who was also churchwarden— came to his aid. He lent Cy his own watch for the time being. It served the purpose equally well, but Cy did not feel comfortable with it. The numerals, the hands, its size and general appearance, seemed strange, and he felt glad to return it to its owner. He counted the days that remained till the expiration of the appointed week; he imagined his precious property in alien hands, its works overhauled by unsympathetic fingers.

Precisely to the day, Cy again appeared at the jeweller's shop, this time before it had closed. To his joy, the watch was done. He saw its interior shine brighter than ever, the flash of the moving escape wheel as the jeweller gave it a final examination, and minor adjustment, in the light of the gas jet. The sight thrilled his whole being.

"It's not a bad old watch," said the jeweller casually. "I wonder if you would care to sell it?" He reached forward a keyless modern production. "See," he added, "I can give you ten shillings and this watch for it. All you have to do, to wind or adjust it, is to turn this knob at the top." He showed Cy how it was done.

Cy was well nigh speechless. His whole being recoiled with dismay at the idea. He shook his head sagely and gasped a deep-drawn "Nooh" that sounded as from his very heart. Somewhat amused, the jeweller smiled. "All right," said he, "I thought perhaps you might be glad to make an exchange." He produced a small cardboard box into which he put Cy's watch on a soft bed of cotton wool. "Three shillings is the fee."

Cy paid the money and, gripping the box, escaped from the shop. He had not felt comfortable amidst those mirrors, those glass cases containing gleaming jewellery and plate. For nothing else than a deep concern for his watch would he have ventured into such a place; he felt thankful to get away with his precious possession safely in his hand, and hoped that never again would he have such an experience, a hope deepened by his reflections on the proffered exchange. "Who knows but what I might never have had it again?" thought he.

The town worried him; he was surrounded with elements foreign to his whole life. He alone was garbed in honest corduroys; boys stared at him as he passed, he heard one remark: "What a funny old man." His heavy boots resounded on the flag pavement, their worn hobnails were unfamiliar with the hardness of its surface, and occasionally he felt like slipping. His one desire was to get right away from the glint and glimmer of it all, back to the friendly darkness of the lanes that led to the village; to feel again the kind yielding turf that skirted the hedges.

The news that Cy had his watch again enlivened the village the following day. The look on his face and his general demeanour supplied its full confirmation. They entered into a friendly conspiracy to all ask him the time; not once, or twice, but often throughout the day. Cy, with unsuspecting ardour, responded to each request, and it was a grand restitution to his lost position. He related his experiences and, with sage expression, accompanied by slight shakes of his head, dwelt at length on the matter of the proffered exchange. They patted him on the back and complimented him on his cuteness; he felt himself one step higher in the estimation of the village.

Thereafter passed the days, the weeks, the months, the years. Springtides, that broke from winter's chills. Summers, with leaves and flowers and song of birds. Autumns, with golden crops—so on till winter's power subdued it all.

Each Sunday, true to time, Cy rang the bells. To normal folk the same routine, year in and out, would have been boredom, yet to him it was replete with joy. Yet not to man can each year give strength to do the self-same task for time on end.

The day came when it was noticeable that Cy was breaking up. His gait was feebler, his triple chimes on Sundays shorter, their rotation erratic. A hefty youth was commissioned to help him; he, with sensitive tact, hovered at his side and in that manner won the old man's confidence. He allowed the youth to ring one bell when chiming, also the "ten minutes" singly; an innovation that had not occurred at that church for forty years past.

The inevitable morning came when Cy, instead of proceeding to church, lay helpless in bed, far too weak to rise. He listened to the ringing of the ten minutes' bell and after that the five minutes. Sentiment had ruled that it would be bad taste to attempt the triple chime whilst the old ringer lay in that condition. The truth dawned on his mind. He asked, "Who will ring the bells when I am gone?" "They won't never be rung so well," was the blunt reply of his attendant.

He lay quiet. The answer had comforted him. To know that throughout life he had rendered a service of value to the community gave him consolation. To believe that they would miss him and remember him with gratitude, gave him joy.

"Tell Ben to call and see me arternoon," he said.

The youth who had helped him appeared. "I was a'listening as ye rang the ten and five," said Cy. "An ye rang um well. An when I be gone I wants ye to take um all on, as you've sin me do."

The youth was genuinely touched. The rural mind is not devoid of sensitive perception; he realized the absolute surrender of self in Cy's request. Struggling with emotion, he blurted: "I'd a sooner ye got well, an took um all on agen, an I'll help ye all I can."

It seemed that with the decline of Cy's strength so did the mists clear from his mind. All who visited him were impressed with his composure and unusual clearness of perception.

"I know well that ye would, boy," said he. "But it seems as if it ain't to be. You must take um all on; all three as I have done. An I shall be lying just outside. Who knows but what I shall hear um ring?"

Another pause, broken by the youth's remark: "I shall never ring um so well as you, Cy."

"Ye maun't say so," answered Cy. "You'll find it ockard at first, but it ull come to ye arter a time. And the watch is to be yourn. You'll hang it on the nail I druv in the wall a'purpose, and it ull gie ye the time to a minute. Keep your bells to that watch, boy, an there won't be no excuse for them as be late."

The Ten-Pointer

By Richard Clapham

It was April in Lakeland. Under the sky-line lay a bowl-shaped hollow, out of which ran a little beck. Below the hollow it prattled amongst the boulders, from whence it fell into a rock-walled ghyll that formed a miniature canyon. Birch and mountain ash trees fringed the ghyll and wide beds of dead brown bracken flattened by the weight of winter snow carpeted the fellside. North of the ghyll the head of the valley formed an amphitheatre where crags and rocks lay in profusion. Here and there in sheltered places on the tops white ribbons of snow still lay awaiting disintegration. Beneath the bracken beds tightly curled heads of new-born fern were starting to appear, but as yet it was early for the parsley ferns, which did not assume their bright green mantles until May. Below the ghyll were scattered thorn trees with here and there a dark green holly.

Between the hollow and the head of the ghyll the beck was flanked by rocky ledges on which grew blaeberry scrub in great profusion. On the lowermost of these ledges a stag was feeding. He carried a ten-point head, with strong, rough horns, and wore a grey-brown jacket of long, thick hair. All winter he had lived in the vicinity of the ghyll, where the trees afforded shelter and there was plenty to eat in the shape of blaeberry, grass and tender shoots of birch and ash. He was a fine beast, a descendant of the old English red deer which in early times inhabited the whole of Lakeland.

As he fed there on the ledge the sun appeared above the fell top and shed its heartening rays o'er crag and ghyll, bathing them in a golden glow. Night creatures departed to their lairs and bird life awoke to greet the day. Having eaten his fill the stag began to climb the fell. He didn't go far, for on reaching a little flat he lay down. With his back to the hill he could scent danger from behind, while in front he had a panoramic view of all the ground below. Bathed in the April sunlight he dozed and chewed the cud.

As the days passed fresh grass began to come and the stag showed signs of wishing to change his quarters. Like others of his kind, he had his wintering place, his summer feeding ground, and his accustomed venue when the autumn rutting time began. One evening he turned his back upon the ghyll, and headed north. For part of his journey he travelled along the still visible line of a Roman road, the pavé of which had long been buried in the grass. After crossing a ghyll by a narrow trod below which lay a precipitous slope, he climbed out to the fell top. As he reached the skyline the sun was setting in the west and the shadows were growing longer. Bathed in the last of the light which still touched the high ground, he stood silhouetted two thousand feet above the darkening dales. Then the last of the golden orb sank from view and he became one with the surrounding gloom.

When the moon rose and flooded the tops with ghostly light, the stag was on his way down a high flat-topped ridge between two valleys. In the dale to the east lay a tarn, while to the west stood a great crag on the wide ledges of which heather and blaeberry grew luxuriously. It was to this crag the stag was heading. Besides good feeding it afforded shelter, and was thus ideal summering ground, for deer love heather, especially young heather that comes after a fire, thus the crag and its environs were particularly attractive to them. Over the ridge on the east side were more crags with grassy slopes above the tarn, so that whichever side the deer chose they were well catered for. Deer, like sheep, need water, especially in hot weather, and they had not far to go to reach the tarn.

In addition to the ten-pointer there were a dozen or more stags in the vicinity of the crag. One or two of them were young beasts, and there were several ancients which had seen their best days. Not long after reaching his new home the ten-pointer dropped one of his horns as he was crossing a ghyll. It fell with a clatter among the rocks. On the following day he lost his other antler. The two cast horns lay far apart for stags seldom drop both antlers at the same spot. Prior to their fall the horns had been attached to short bony protuberances or pedicles on the stag's skull. Directly they became detached the skin and epidermis surrounding the pedicles closed over the tops of the latter and a new growth of bone began. This was in the form of cartilage and gristle, and it was covered by a hairy skin known as the velvet. Through this velvet ran nerves which made the growing antlers touchy, thus the stag took care to keep them clear of exterior objects. One day he had a difference of opinion with another stag, but instead of charging head on at his adversary he rose up on his hind legs and hit at his opponent with his forefeet, the hooves of which could inflict painful blows. These cervine boxing matches were of brief duration, very different from the battles which took place in autumn. The stags cast their horns at different times according to their age, the older beasts being first to lose their headgear. Thus in the band which inhabited the crag you could see some stags with both horns, some with one antler, and others that were bald-headed.

As summer advanced the sun gained power, rocks and stones felt warm to the touch and the cool water of the tarn became inviting to both deer and sheep. One hot day the ten-pointer and two other stags walked knee-deep into the shallows where they drank. As they raised their dripping muzzles the falling drops were like diamonds in the sunlight. Having drunk their fill they stood there for a while. Not far away an ewe and her lambs slaked their thirst.

As the days passed the ten-pointer's horns slowly developed. The beam of the antler grew longer and points branched from it. All the stags were in velvet, some of their horns being more advanced than others. The deer spent most of their time feeding and resting. Their meal times were at dusk and dawn. During the day they lay in their beds chewing the cud and dozing. When overcome by sleep the ten-pointer stretched his head and

neck on the ground or lay curled up like a fox. Always amongst
the band of stags were some that kept on the alert. Even when
dozing they had one eye open for possible danger. They were
finicky in their feeding habits. Coarse grass that suited cattle
made no appeal to them. They had a preference for certain
tit-bits which grew here and there, and as they picked them they
kept moving on. Their table manners were most polite. There
was no jostling or grabbing.

Day after day the sun glared down from a brassy sky and
the land was parched. Grass and young heather that grew
where a thin layer of peat soil overlaid the rock became burned
and the water-courses on the fellsides dried up. Luckily for
the deer the tarn relieved their thirst, but the country as a
whole cried out for rain. It came at last when dark clouds
gathered and thunder rumbled in the distance. Gradually the
mutterings grew louder and the sky was split by a vivid flash
of lightning. Then the sky opened and great drops of rain
splashed amongst the rocks. These were followed by a deluge
that came hissing down in an almost solid wall of water. As
the rain fell, lightning flashed incessantly and the roar of the
thunder was awe inspiring as it reverberated amongst the crags.
Down every ghyll and runner brown columns of water poured,
looking like snakes as they wound their way amongst the
stones. Traversing the empty stream beds they merged with
the water of the tarn where the brown flood spread out and
coloured the surface.

During the downpour the ten-pointer turned his tail to the
storm and stood in the half shelter of a rock. Gradually the
thunder died to a distant mutter, the rain ceased, and the sun
broke through the clouds. On the fellsides the brown snakes
of water changed to silver ribbons that dashed swiftly down their
rocky beds, and the grass steamed in the heat. Raindrops
glistened like myriad diamonds and the air felt fresh and clear.

Bathed in sunlight the ten-pointer left his shelter and shook
himself. For an instant he was enveloped in a haze of flying
drops that flashed like a heliograph. Despite the heavy downpour he was practically dry. He had shed his winter coat and
wore his summer garb of glossy bright bay hair, that merged
into the grey on his face and legs.

The horns which he had shed in April bore brow, bay and
tray points with a fork on each top. Now two additional points

were appearing on his new antlers. Instead of forks both tops bore tridents or cups which made him a twelve-pointer, otherwise a royal. He thus carried the typical headgear of an adult wild stag. His horns were still in velvet, but their length and spread gave promise of an outstanding head in the near future.

After the rain the parched fellside took a new lease of life. Already from beneath the dead winter bracken had sprung a fresh green growth. The beds of fern were in places tall enough to hide a man, and amongst the rocks the clumps of parsley fern added a touch of brighter green. From the slopes above the tarn came a continuous chirping of grasshoppers, and here and there on the sun-warmed stones brown lizards lay enjoying the heat. They looked lethargic, but when you tried to catch them they disappeared like magic amongst the grass. Above the crags swifts screamed through the air in ceaseless pursuit of insects. Tireless fliers, they never rested, seeming to have learnt the art of perpetual motion. Towards dusk they rose higher and higher until they finally faded from human ken. What they did up there no man can tell.

Sometimes at dawn or dusk a fox appeared amongst the rocks, either returning from its nightly foray or setting forth upon a hunting expedition. They were big brutes some of these foxes, real old-timers, long-legged and silvery coated. They lived far up amongst the crags, where they lay by day on the heather-covered ledges or in wild weather amongst the subterranean passages under the piled-up boulders. Often in the more lonely dales they wandered about during the daytime.

Now and then a stoat came bounding along the fellside, its black-tipped tail waving behind it. Small as they were, the stoats loved killing. They lived on rabbits, mice and any birds that they could catch. In winter on the high ground they turned white with the exception of their black tail-tips. A white stoat amongst snow is well camouflaged, but occasionally an ermine could be seen on bare ground where it was very conspicuous. Stoats regularly hunted the stone walls. Rabbits lay in the wall bottoms and the stoats were well aware of the fact.

The ten-pointer, which had now become a royal, completed his horn growth in July. The velvet which covered his antlers then became necrotic and set up irritation. This made the stag rub his horns on rocks and other objects, thus causing the velvet to peel off in strips. Beneath it the bone was white, but on exposure to the air it darkened, and in the royal's case turned nearly black. As he stood there on the fellside he looked a perfect picture of a stag. He carried a glorious head with twelve white-tipped needle-sharp tines. His horns were nearly three feet long, thick in the beam, and beautifully pearled. That these branching antlers should have been grown in the short space of between four and five months was one of nature's miracles. Fat with summer feed, he was in grand condition, and his bay coat shone glossy in the sunlight.

August arrived, and with it came colour that turned the heather into a sea of purple. Amongst the band of stags all heads were clear of velvet. Some horns were dark in colour, others of lighter shade. The roughest antlers tended to show the darkest tints.

Towards the middle of September the royal showed signs of restlessness. He visited the flat-topped ridge and rolled in the pools which lay amongst the peat hags. Gone was his glossy hair, for when he rose from his bath his coat dripped peaty batter. Came a bodily change, too. His neck began to swell, and the long hairs which covered it stood out like a great ruff. What, you may ask, was the reason for his behaviour? The answer is, sex.

Gradually with all the stags the breeding impulse was coming to a head. The time had arrived for them to change their ground again and migrate to their accustomed rutting place, where they would mate with hinds.

One evening the royal left his summer home, sank the hill and, after rounding the end of the tarn, climbed out towards the opposite skyline. When he reached it he was momentarily silhouetted in the last rays of the setting sun, then, as the light faded, he headed north. Keeping to the undulating skyline he travelled on with the short crisp grass of the tops beneath his feet. Darkness fell and for a time he merged with the gloom. Then the moon rose and the fell was bathed in silvery light. Behind the rocks and walls black shadows lay while that of the stag moved with him.

At long last he came to a place where he looked down upon two valleys with a tongue or ridge between. The scent of deer hung in the air, for other stags were there before him, and they smelled strongly, as is their nature during the period of the rut. Amongst the stags on the faintly illuminated ground below were bunches of hinds. These formed the magnet that was drawing the outlying stags towards the autumn rendezvous.

As the royal strode down the slopes towards the ridge a roar shattered the silence of the night. It shook the earth and ended with a series of deep, coughing grunts. The author of it was an eight-pointer which had rounded up some hinds and was proclaiming to all and sundry that the said hinds formed his own particular harem. I don't know what the royal thought, but he saw the stag and at once took up the challenge. Opening his mouth he, too, let out a roar that ended in a series of lion-like grunts. His coat was black with rolling in the peat, and with bloodshot eyes and swollen neck he looked a most determined customer. Nothing loath, the eight-pointer strode out to meet him. After manœuvring for position a battle began there in the moonlight. The royal, wise in his generation, secured an uphill stance that favoured his attack. They met head-on with a crash and rattle of antlers that developed into a strenuous pushing match. Shoving and grunting, their hooves churned up the peat as they struggled for mastery. At last the royal's weight began to tell, and his enemy gave ground. Recovering himself, the eight-pointer got clear, and then for some minutes they faced each other like two strange dogs. Then at it they went again, and once more the royal's weight helped him to score. For an instant the eight-pointer was on his knees, but a desperate effort saved him. Strive as he would he was outfought, and at last he was obliged to disengage. As he did so the royal drove in and scored his flank with a horn point. That was the end. The eight-pointer turned and fled. The royal chased him for some distance, then swung back towards the hinds. Roaring defiance, he drove off a younger stag that had the cheek to approach his harem, and then he roared again, a challenge to any would-be suitors.

For a time he was cock of the walk, and then a nine-pointer butted in. He suffered the same fate as his predecessor, leaving the royal triumphant. The latter was master stag without a doubt, for no other beast came forward to test his mettle. What with his amours and pursuit of any stag that drew too near his hinds the royal led a strenuous life. He had no time to eat or sleep, and his exertions began to tell on even his strong constitution. Daily he grew thinner and more tucked-up until at last he was fain to call a halt and leave his harem to the younger stags, which were forever trying to encroach upon his ladies.

Tired and worn out he bethought him of his winter quarters near the ghyll and one afternoon he headed south.

His sense of direction took him unerringly across the mist-covered tops, and at long last he turned downhill and found himself in the bowl-shaped hollow above the ghyll. As he slowly descended towards the trees he emerged below the mist curtain, where on the old familiar ground he settled down to pass the dreary winter months and await the coming of another Spring.